THE CHRISTIAN WEDDING PLANNER

RUTH MUZZY AND R. KENT HUGHES

CHERYL S. HASTINGS, EDITOR

TYNDALE HOUSE PUBLISHERS, INCORPORATED
WHEATON, ILLINOIS

All Scripture quotations are taken from the *King James Version* unless otherwise indicated.

ISBN 0-8423-0253-0
Copyright © 1984 by Ruth Muzzy and R. Kent Hughes
Printed in the United States of America

8   9   10   11   12   13   93   92   91   90   89

◆ ACKNOWLEDGMENTS ◆

With appreciation we acknowledge and thank those who gave of their time, suggestions, and information. We are grateful!

Cheryl Hastings, with her impelling spirit and knack for organization, was of enormous help in the writing of this book.

We would also like to express our gratitude

TO Dr. Stewart Odell, obstetrician/gynecologist, for contributing to the chapter, "Intimacy and the Honeymoon"

TO the Reverend Larry Fullerton for his assistance with the premarital counseling material

TO Reginald R. Gerig, organist and music adviser for weddings for more than thirty years

TO Rhoella Tillman, home economist

TO Carol Erickson, educator and wedding coordinator

TO Jim VanEwyk of Pfund and Clint Florists, Elmhurst, Illinois

TO Dorothy Ronzheimer and other friends who were full of new ideas

TO Nancy Nehmer and the others at Tyndale House for their part in the making of this book

TO our spouses and family who gave immeasurable encouragement.

We thank God for the opportunity to share with all of you the information and insights He has given us through the many years of organizing weddings.

You have met that special someone, gotten to know and love him, and now you're engaged. Enjoy your engagement! Share the intimacies of your hearts with each other.

Most important of all, engagement is a time of preparation for your marriage. But it is also the time to plan your wedding ceremony.

Every bride-to-be approaches her wedding day with a good measure of excitement as well as apprehension. And both of these emotions are present for good reason! You are preparing to join your life to another's and you want that once-in-a-lifetime occasion to be flawless.

You are beginning a new chapter of your life—and each page's experiences will be shared by your new husband. You can't wait to learn everything about him, and share all that you are with him. You have found a most treasured friend, and that is reason to be excited! Your longing for a beautiful and meaningful wedding is uppermost in your thinking.

But in order to have a worshipful wedding ceremony, many decisions must be made. Where do you begin? There is a date to be set, a photographer to be chosen, invitations to be ordered . . . the list goes on and on! So, you see, it is understandable for a bride to be apprehensive, too. BUT, it is not *necessary!*

We want to invite you to let us help you and the others involved get organized. Instead of darting here and there jotting down notes on the backs of envelopes, use the handy schedules, checklists, and worksheets we've included inside. (And feel free to duplicate them when necessary.) Garnering ideas from our experience with countless weddings, we present some basic guidelines—not a set of rigid rules, but valuable, practical ways to manage the many details of planning a Christian wedding.

As much as possible, this book has been designed to deal with the different aspects of planning in the order that you should approach them. But we suggest that you read it *all the way through* once; it's best if you have the whole picture in mind and know some of the decisions that you will have to face in the near future. Then focus in on each decision, chapter by chapter, as you come to it. If you use the checklists and schedules, you will be able to enjoy that special day to its fullest. And it should be your day to enjoy!

Through this book we hope to provide help, both in understanding the meaning behind the ceremony and in planning the wedding itself.

Our congratulations and very best wishes to you for a wonderful celebration.

Ruth Muzzy
R. Kent Hughes

CHAPTER ONE

Christian Marriage

WHY A CHRISTIAN WEDDING SERVICE?

Since couples who have been married by a justice of the peace or a ship's captain are just as married as those who have had a church wedding, this question is fair to ask. The answer comes easily— and is exhilarating for the one who believes in Jesus Christ.

The basic reason a Christian ceremony is proper for the believer is that marriage in Christ is more than a mere contract. The early Christians understood something that is often forgotten today—that marriage is a *unio mystica*, a mystical union. They saw marriage as the creation of a profound unity of two individual people. Since believers are already united in Christ, marriage brings about the greatest of unions. It is the spiritual union which gives an added depth to marriage, and this depth of relationship makes a distinctly Christian wedding ceremony very appropriate.

Christians also realize that marriage was instituted by God in the original creation order. According to Genesis 2, God declared all creation good—except for one aspect. "Then the Lord God said, 'It is not good for the man to be alone; I will make him a helper suitable for him' "

(Gen. 2:18, NASB). Thus, God created marriage. Christ Himself honored marriage by performing His first public miracle at the marriage in Cana of Galilee (Jn. 2:1-11). God celebrates believers' marriages and so should His people.

A Christian wedding ceremony is most natural for believers because it publicly displays the deepest of commitments. It gives the couple an opportunity to declare before family and friends their lifelong devotion, and thus invite the support and prayers of their Christian brothers and sisters. It also gives the Christian community the opportunity to publicly approve and support the marriage.

The image of the bride, radiant in her white dress, and the image of the groom, lovingly at her side, provide a marvelous symbol of Christ and the Church. One day Christ will "present to Himself the church in all her glory, having no spot or wrinkle" (Eph. 5:27, NASB). This unique symbolism in itself is reason enough to have a Christian ceremony.

CHRISTIAN MARRIAGE IS A REDEMPTIVE RELATIONSHIP

Marriage is meant to gradually help a couple become what God created them to be—Christlike. In this sense, it is redemptive.

The Apostle Paul emphasized this point when he said to husbands, "Husbands, love your wives, just as Christ also loved the church and gave Himself up for her" (Eph. 5:25, NASB). Actually, this also is the way wives are to love their husbands, for all believers are to love as Christ did.

Three words help us understand Christ's redemptive love for the Church: incarnation, death, and intercession. Through marriage, Christians are meant to experience something of each of these three elements, thus becoming more like Christ.

Christian Marriage Involves Incarnation

The word "incarnation" refers to God taking on human flesh. When Jesus came to us, He came in a human body. Because He did this, He experienced everything we experience. Jesus knew what it was like to be human; He knew the joys of holding a newborn baby, the sweat of human toil and drudgery, and the pain of rejection. Thus He was a man who could understand our feelings of weakness. Hebrews 4:15 says, "For we do not have a high priest who cannot sympathize with our weaknesses, but one who has been tempted in all things as we are, yet without sin" (NASB).

So, too, marriage calls us to live "incarnationally" with our spouse; that is, to understand and feel what life is like for someone else—to be a part of another's hurts and joys. As we do this, we act as Christ acted. Marriage pushes husbands and wives toward the experience of incarnation. This helps to restore people to what God made them to be.

Christian Marriage Involves Death

The second great characteristic of Christ's love is His death. He died for us, His beloved.

Marriage gives husbands and wives the opportunity to "die" for one another. Of course, this does not mean that those who are married pay for one another's sins. It simply means marriage brings continuing opportunities for each spouse to give up his or her own desires for the sake of the other. Such daily "dying" is redemptive, and helps the couple to become more of what God intended.

Christian Marriage Involves Intercessory Prayer

The third aspect of Christ's love is that He is always praying for the Church. This means He is always speaking on our behalf. His prayers are perfect because He understands what we are going through (see Hebrews 4:15).

Christian marriage is meant to produce men and women who pray with a real understanding of each other, the way Christ does.

In summary, then, we become what God intended us to be when we can truly understand the person we have chosen to marry, when we give up our own desires for the good of the other, and when we can pray with a clear knowledge of the other person's feelings and thoughts. Our spouse is allowed to become what he was intended to be through our prayers, understanding, and giving of ourselves.

Engagement

After your parents and your groom's parents have agreed to your wishes to marry, you may want to send a small gift or bouquet of flowers to your fiancé's mother and father. Include a note expressing your joy in anticipation of joining their family.

ANNOUNCEMENT PARTY

One way to celebrate your engagement is for your parents to give a party to announce the news to your close friends and relatives. It should be given before the information appears in the newspaper. If you like, your mother can invite people over to meet your "friend," and then your father can reveal the "inside facts." Otherwise, your mother could write informal notes or send purchased invitations for a party in honor of the two of you. Of course, there is nothing wrong with hosting your own party, either.

Some miscellaneous details:

1. If you have a dinner party and can locate small pictures of each of you alone or both of you together, you might have extra prints made and glue them to place cards.
2. Plan a little speech ahead of time to accept all of the good wishes you will

be getting. If you have received your ring, have it on display.
3. A personal note of thanks should be written to anyone who gives a gift at this time.

Notes or phone calls to your close friends and relatives could be another way of letting people know of your engagement. Also, a brief visit to grandparents or special people would fill them in on the rumors they may have been hearing.

Employee news sheets and/or church papers are effective ways of spreading the news, also.

NEWSPAPER ANNOUNCEMENT

Your mother may take the responsibility for seeing that your engagement is announced in the newspaper. If she does, have her send a copy of the information to the groom's mother if she lives at another location. If there is more than one newspaper in the area, ask for the announcements to be released on the same day, if possible. Wherever and whenever it *is* announced, it should be issued in your parents' name.

The local newspaper should provide a

form to be filled out with the information they need, such as:

- The full name and address of the bride and groom
- What schools both have attended; professional training, and/or major fields of study
- Current occupations
- The names of both sets of parents
- Where the wedding will take place
- A general idea of when the wedding will take place (unless no date has been set)
- Hometowns of both the bride and groom
- Military service
- Names of both sets of grandparents (if they live in the area)

Make sure the names are spelled correctly, and no nicknames are used.

If you would like to write it as you wish it to appear in the paper, type all the information, double spaced, on an 8½" x 11" sheet of white paper. Submit this early in the week if you want it published in a Sunday paper. The date you want this information released may be written in the upper right-hand corner of the form, with the name and telephone number of a person who can verify all of the information. If you mail it to the paper, put your name and return address on the envelope.

If you like, include a 5" x 7" glossy black-and-white print of you or you and your fiancé. It will reproduce better if the background is plain and light. Send a color picture only if it is very bright and clear. Generally, newspapers prefer that you not write on the back of the picture. It will not be returned, but often you may pick it up if you like. If you send it in the mail, be sure to place it between cardboard.

Once the announcement has been published you can usually get extra copies of this edition of the newspaper to add to your wedding keepsakes.

If there has been a recent death in the family, your engagement announcement should not appear in the paper.

Special Wording
When one of your parents is deceased, the word "late" always precedes his or her name. Whether the announcement is made by your father or mother, the same wording is used. Here is an example for when the father is deceased:

*Mrs. Philip Smith announces
the engagement
of her daughter, Miss Emily Smith,
to Mr. Lester Jones . . .
Miss Smith is also the daughter
of the late Philip Smith.*

When the bride's mother has married again, both she and her present husband may announce it. The phrase, "also the daughter of the late . . ." is included. When the bride's father has married again, his name is usually used alone, unless his present wife has been an integral part of the bride's life. Again, the phrase, "also the daughter of the late . . ." is included.

When the bride's parents are both deceased, the closest relative or friend makes the announcement.

In the case of divorce, both parents have claims on their daughter, so it is important to acknowledge both of them. If the mother has not remarried, she announces the engagement. The phrase, "also the daughter of Mr. . . ." is included. Sometimes, the announcement is issued in both names with an "and" between their full names.

If the mother has remarried, she and her spouse may announce the engagement and the phrase "also the daughter of Mr. . . ." is included. In the event that the father makes the announcement, the mother should be acknowledged in the same way.

If the bride is adopted, that fact need not be mentioned, unless she has retained her own name. If the bride is divorced, or widowed, the engagement is not announced in the paper, unless she is a celebrity; nor is a second time engagement usually announced.

CHAPTER THREE

Thinking Things Through

A wedding is a time for you and your groom to commit yourselves to a life together. It reflects the hope and excitement shared by you and your groom; it is a very personal occasion. But while you will make many of the final decisions, remember that family, friends, and professionals can offer helpful advice.

Some families have particular traditions that have been carried on from generation to generation, involving the whole family. Others simply expect correct etiquette and formality to be followed without question. There is no written law stating what should or should not be done, but it may be wise to take into consideration local customs and parents' desires. A church will usually have its own rules also, but may grant permission for variations.

A family gathering is a good time to share ideas about how your wedding and reception might be handled. Also, during this time, family members can gain a clearer understanding of the differing parts you would like them to play.

Many emotions come to the surface as the date approaches and your wedding plans take shape. Everyone involved will be excited, yet your parents may think they are about to lose their "little girl." At the same time, you may have your own uncertainties about the future. Taking your parents' suggestions into consideration may relieve a portion of everyone's inner struggles. This will let them know that their help is appreciated. However, there may come a point when you will need gracefully to assert yourself as the final decision maker. Your wedding day will be special for many people, but it will be impossible to please everyone. Think of this time as an opportunity to sharpen your decision-making and organizing skills—skills which will last you a lifetime.

Your groom will want to be involved, but may not want the hassle of all the little details. He may simply say, "Do it the way you want." Either way, involve him as much as possible in major decisions, and listen to him. Make a list of things that you think he might like to do, and let him choose those he has time for. Settle on a deadline, and trust him to accomplish what he has agreed to do.

You have already been thinking about some of the important decisions that must be made. How do you start? Here are some suggestions.

DECISION I: THE SETTING

A variety of factors must be taken into consideration when deciding the setting and formality of your wedding. Some of these are the size of the wedding, your budget, family traditions, and the availability of your preferred location.

Again and again we come back to the church because that is the traditional location for a Christ-honoring ceremony. If you have a church home, you will most likely feel comfortable having your ceremony there because you are familiar with the style of worship and the people who attend there. Even if the church is small, your ceremony can still be memorable and Christ-honoring.

A public place, such as a banquet facility, hotel, or country club, may be a necessity if you have a large guest list and no other location can handle your wedding. For any of these locations, an organ may be rented and brought in, or other musicians may be hired. Your florist can still set up any flowers, greenery, and candles that you order.

A wedding that takes place in someone's home will probably be a small, intimate affair unless the home is large enough to accommodate more guests. The formality of dress for this atmosphere is up to you. Many of our grandparents were married in this relaxed manner.

A garden or outdoor wedding among the freshness of new flowers and natural greenery can be a pleasant experience. There are several factors to think about beforehand, though. Will you have to deal with any nearby highway noise or with air traffic overhead? Should the area be sprayed for bugs a few days prior to the ceremony? If the weather is bad that day, what alternative will there be? (It's a good idea to rent a tent for the wedding and reception so everyone may relax in the shade.)

DECISION II: THE AVAILABILITY OF PEOPLE AND THE CHURCH

If you do decide upon a church wedding, be sure to contact your minister and the church right away in order to check the minister's schedule and the church calendar. If you are given a variety of dates that he and the church are available, your choice will be easy. This will also make reserving a reception site easier (if you are considering someplace other than the church hall). You may also want to clear your date with family and special friends.

If for some reason, you are limited to having your wedding on one particular date, the rest of your plans will obviously need to work around this date.

DECISION III: THE NUMBER OF GUESTS

The number of guests you invite to your wedding may need to be determined by the size of the church or reception site. Or it may work the other way around, depending upon your priorities. Also, you will need to consider how many guests you can *afford* to invite before establishing your guest list. Remember that the number of guests affects the time you will spend addressing invitations, the time you will spend standing in the receiving line, and the time involved in writing thank-you notes later, too. Also, it's helpful to realize that usually one-fourth to one-third of the invited guests will not be able to attend the wedding and reception.

DECISION IV: THE BUDGET

Traditionally, the bride's parents have footed the bill for the wedding ceremony and reception. Sometimes both sets of parents agree to share the expense, in which case the budget should be discussed openly. But if you and your groom are paying, remember you will not want the wedding to put you in debt for your first year of marriage. The best thing to do is to set an appropriate budget and *stick to it*. (Be sure to read the following chapter for more specific guidelines on budgeting.)

It's very difficult to predict what the entire wedding expense will be. Avoid charges that are larger than you can realistically afford. Both your pocketbook and future peace of mind are important. Don't try to make anyone else's dreams come true or try to create the social event of the year, either. Decide what you want, and be firm with your convictions. Don't be intimidated by those who mean well but say, "You must do it like everyone else."

Priorities

To help you avoid this temptation of overspending, here is a suggestion: Before you do anything else, take pencil and paper and list your priorities in order of importance. Ask yourself, "Do I want a sit-down dinner reception?" "Is it important to have that dress designed by Priscilla of Boston?" "Are numerous flowers and decorations a must for this special day?" "Do I want to purchase any special clothes for the honeymoon?" "What do we need to purchase for our new home?"

Take advantage of the space below to list some of your "musts."

1. _____
2. _____
3. _____
4. _____
5. _____
6. _____
7. _____
8. _____

A WORD ABOUT CONTRACTS

A written contract is very important for many of the transactions you are about to make. Most places will have their own, but if not, you can draft one yourself by writing your name and address at the top of a sheet of paper, and then stating the date, time, product, and price agreed upon. Sign your name on the paper, and have the other person sign it also. When someone gives you details over the phone, send him a letter immediately confirming what was discussed.

If you have done this and a mistake occurs, write or call the other party immediately. Refer to the contract, and ask for a refund or an adjustment.

As you can see, there are many decisions that will need to be made, but you have already made one decision—to marry and thus conform to the guidelines that God has given concerning marriage. Why not start by asking His blessing on your new beginning, and His guidance for your marriage plans?

CHAPTER FOUR

Budgeting

Often we wish for some magical word that will make the matter of budgeting disappear. It might be fun to have everything your heart could possibly want for your wedding without thought for expense. But the matter of budgeting *does* exist, and eventually it *does* need to be discussed. It can be exciting and challenging to figure out ways of making your dream wedding happen, whatever the amount of funds you have. Even if financial arrangements for a wedding are not a problem, it is best to work out a budget for all the expenditures, and then to watch for the best values for your money.

One of the oldest wedding traditions is that of the bride and her parents paying for the wedding. Traditionally, the bride's parents are the ones who have the final say concerning the guest list and formality of the wedding and are usually the host and hostess for the reception. They provide for the bride's clothing needs, the flowers, the photographs, the church, and much more. Most parents consider it a privilege to have this honor. More recently, however, the bride and groom often offer to share in the expenses of their own wedding.

Possibly your family is unable or unwilling to pay for the wedding. If this is the case and your groom and his family offer monetary assistance, you may accept it if you so desire. Sometimes a relative or close friend will want to be useful in this regard also. If this is acceptable with everyone else involved, the arrangements should be discussed openly so that everyone understands the guidelines and what particular part they will play. If no assistance is available, then your family should proceed with whatever money they have and tailor the guest list and reception accordingly.

If you find yourself in the situation of wanting to get married but your parents are in another country or are deceased, the groom's parents may step in and make the necessary provisions. Other conditions in which the groom's parents could pay for the wedding and reception would be if the two families are distantly related or are very old friends. If your parents are living, the invitation should still be issued in the names of your parents even if the groom's parents give the wedding.

When planning a budget, take into consideration first those items that you listed as "musts" in the preceding chapter. They may be the location of the ceremony, reception refreshments, the services of a particular photographer or florist, or the music. Each person has different priorities. Using the accompanying chart, overestimate each item according to your preferences and then add up the round figure. If the grand total is over what you had in mind, then cut out those items you can do without. If your budget allows for a few more items, then you may add those things that you had previously excluded. As a rule, plan on the flowers taking up about 15 to 25 percent of your budget. The reception usually takes up the largest portion of the total—probably 50 percent of your funds.

If your parents do not care to make a commitment of a definite amount, but say, "Just go ahead and use your own judgment," it would be wise to survey the style in which your family lives, or the customs of your friends and relatives, and choose accordingly. You should feel comfortable with the decisions you make, and know that whoever is paying should be able to live with the bills when the wedding is over.

Avoid the trauma of having a huge debt after the wedding. One way to prevent this is to do some "price shopping" and get estimates over the phone. Then discuss your findings with your parents or those who are paying the bills. You will soon realize their expectations.

If you want your budget to balance in the end, you must make a rough estimate of how much money is available and how it is to be spent. (But be sure to design your budget in such a way that it is flexible enough to handle unexpected expenses.) Every expense should be itemized; there is no way around this. It may be helpful for you to know that most of your wedding and reception expenditures will be on a cash basis. Expect to give downpayments for clothing, the reception site, the cake, and several other items. Keep track of those downpayments on the specified worksheet in this chapter.

ADDING IT ALL UP

	Cost	
	ESTIMATED	ACTUAL*
Ceremony expenses (church, pastor, etc.)	$250 +	_____
Reception (cake, food)	_____	_____
Florist	150	_____
Photographer	275	_____
Invitations	_____	_____
Attire (wedding dress, trousseau)	_____	_____
Gifts (for wedding party)	_____	_____
Transportation	_____	_____
Appointments (medical)	_____	_____
Accommodations	_____	_____
Miscellaneous	_____	_____
Total	$_____	_____

*(Gather from expense forms in other chapters.)

DOWNPAYMENTS

	AMOUNT	DATE PAID
Your dress	$_____	_____
Bridesmaids' dresses	_____	_____
Invitations	_____	_____
Flowers	_____	_____
Cake	_____	_____
Photographer	_____	_____
Reception	_____	_____
Caterer	_____	_____
Church arrangements	_____	_____
Musicians	_____	_____

FINANCIAL RESPONSIBILITIES

Everyone involved in the planning of your wedding will have definite financial responsibilities. This applies to you and your family as well as to your groom and his family. On the other hand, there are some responsibilities which can go either way and will need to be decided upon between the two families.

If both you and your groom have good jobs, *you* may decide to take on all of the expenses of the wedding together, or you may ask both sets of parents to take on certain expenses. Whatever the arrangements, everything will work out better if all those involved have an attitude of appreciation toward the others. This could cement interfamily relationships for many years to come.

Below is a list of who is responsible for what. If both families decide to switch responsibilities, that would be fine, as long as each family has a clear understanding of the expectations of the other.

FINANCIAL RESPONSIBILITIES

BRIDE AND HER FAMILY

Announcement party and engagement photo for the paper

Groom's ring*

Her blood test, medical and dental examinations*

Her car check-up and insurance*

Health insurance*

Bride's wedding dress, veil and accessories

Bridesmaids' dresses and accessories (This expense is often assumed by the attendants.)

Her family's personal attire for wedding festivities

Wedding gift for groom*

Gifts for maid of honor and bridesmaids*

Gift for her parents (optional)*

Gifts for hostesses of parties (optional)*

GROOM AND HIS FAMILY

Bride's engagement and wedding rings*

His blood test, medical and dental examinations*

His car check-up and insurance*

Health insurance*

Groom's wedding attire

Rental of wedding attire for best man, groomsmen and ushers (This expense is often assumed by the attendants.)

His family's personal attire for wedding festivities

Wedding gift for bride*

Gifts for best man, groomsmen and ushers*

Gift for his parents (optional)*

BRIDE AND HER FAMILY

Invitations, announcements, enclosures, and postage

Trousseau of clothes and lingerie for bride

Trousseau of linens, china, silver, crystal, or furniture for the bride and groom (optional)

Bridesmaids' luncheon

Wedding ceremony expenses:
rental fees, custodian, organist, soloist, choir, candles, candelabra, aisle runner, kneeling bench, marquee or awning for church entrance, other equipment

Flowers:
decorations for church, bouquets and headdresses for all attendants, flowers for friends who help at the wedding or reception, corsages for grandmothers

Photos before and after the wedding, candids, movies, recordings, album
(This expense may be shared by the bride and groom and both parents.)

Traveling expenses and hotel bills for her family

Accommodations for the bride's family and the bride's attendants

Accommodations for out-of-town members of the wedding party and receiving line (optional)
(They are the guests of the bride and her family.)

GROOM AND HIS FAMILY

Marriage license*

Bachelor get-together

Rehearsal dinner

Flowers:
bride's bouquet and corsages for mothers, boutonnieres for male attendants, going-away corsage for bride*
(These should be ordered by the bride and the bill sent to the groom before the wedding.)
(Sometimes the groom pays for all of the flowers for the wedding party.)

Fee or honorarium for minister or other official, also for second person officiating*

Traveling expenses for groom and his family

Accommodations for the groom's family, the best man and ushers

BRIDE AND HER FAMILY

(Accommodations should be made at her home, with friends, or at a hotel.)

Transportation of the bride and bridal party to the church and the reception (limousine or carriage)

Expenses involved with the arranging of gifts for display, insurance, and a guard for gifts during rehearsal and wedding activities

All expenses of reception:
rental fees, food, beverage, services, flowers, decorations, gratuities, cake, musicians, photos, other expenses

After the reception there is often a light buffet served to the wedding party and out-of-town relatives before the bride and groom leave on their trip
(This may also be done in the form of a brunch the next morning.)

GROOM AND HIS FAMILY

Transportation of the groom and groomsmen to the church

Honeymoon*

Future home and major equipment*

Expense of shipping wedding presents*

Any other expenses they elect to assume

*It would be reasonable to expect the bride and groom to assume these expenses themselves if they are financially able to do so.

BUDGETING YOUR TIME

Not only does budgeting your money make your plans easier, but budgeting your time will help as well. Take into consideration all of the different demands on your time coming up in the next few months before your wedding. The Engagement Calendar in chapter 16 will help you do this. Then make a schedule for each day, blocking out the times you spend at your job, school, church, recreation, sleeping, etc. Prioritize the things that need to be done, and then place them in the open time slots accordingly. Include such details as meetings, shopping, and any other activities. By doing this you will find that you can accomplish a great deal more in one day than you had expected!

Finally, be happy with the decisions you have made and the boundaries you have set for yourself. Ask the Lord for His blessings and guidance on all your plans, and then believe that He will give them.

EXPENSE GUIDE FOR GROOM AND FAMILY

	Cost				Cost	
	ESTIMATED	ACTUAL			ESTIMATED	ACTUAL
Engagement ring	$	200	Attire		$	
Wedding ring			Accommodations			
Flowers			Rehearsal dinner			
Bride's bouquet			Honorarium			
Bride's going-away corsage			Marriage license			
Bride's mother's corsage			Honeymoon			
Groom's mother's corsage			Reception or open house (if from out-of-town)			
Boutonnieres			Other			
Other						
Gifts						
Bride						
Best man						
Other men						
Ring bearer						
Parents (optional)			**Total**	$		

The Minister & Premarital Counseling

THE INITIAL VISIT

You must take the initiative in arranging a visit with your minister. As you do so, keep two things in mind. One, you are the one asking for *his* time, so he should tell you what time is best for him. (*You* should be willing to rearrange your schedule to be able to meet with him, although most pastors will be accommodating.) Two, both you and your fiancé should attend the meeting. If only one of you shows up, the minister will probably reschedule the appointment, thus wasting his time and yours.

Often busy pastors leave their scheduling with their secretaries. Therefore, instead of setting up the appointment as you shake the minister's hand Sunday morning, it is better to call his secretary during the week.

Many churches ask the engaged couple to complete a precounseling questionnaire or an application for marriage. If you are asked to fill these out, the secretary will tell you how to do so.

If the minister plans to discuss the wedding ceremony details during your first appointment, then you will want to be prepared. Read the chapter on Ceremony Specifics for examples of the orders of service for different denominations, and

other helpful advice. Also, be prepared to talk when the appointment begins, since you will most likely be given only thirty to forty minutes.

Unless the minister knows you and your fiancé well, it must be understood that the minister will ask you some personal questions before promising his participation in the wedding. Expect him to question both of you about your commitment to Christ. Before he will preside at a wedding, a minister of the gospel would like to know that both of the participants can truly say they know Christ. Moreover, experienced pastors know that the level of commitment to Christ should be similar for both marriage partners. The combination of a deeply committed Christian and a lukewarm Christian often means a troubled future.

Prospective couples can also expect to be questioned about what their families think of the proposed marriage. Do they wholeheartedly approve, or do they have reservations? The answers to these questions are very important to caring ministers.

Couples can be sure that they will be asked about their long-range professional goals and life goals. Compatibility of direction is very important to the careful counselor. Questions about your current financial responsibility and future plans are commonly asked. If there has been a former marriage, the couple must come fully prepared to discuss the past in detail.

Such discussions are not always easy. However, you and your fiancé should not regard these questions as impositions. Instead, think of them as the honest concern of a minister who has been charged by God to care for you. He would be an unfaithful servant if he avoided such probing.

When the pastor gives his approval, the rehearsal and wedding dates should be confirmed on the church calendar. At this meeting, you may also arrange for further premarital counseling and discussion of the wedding ceremony.

THE HONORARIUM

It is proper to ask the clergyman privately how much the typical wedding honorarium is. Some clergymen do not receive honorariums, and that gives them the opportunity to tell you so. Others have a standard fee. If you give the clergyman an honorarium, it should be done *privately*. (The groom should take care of this payment. See "Financial Responsibilities" in chapter 4.)

USE OF OTHER CLERGY

While most ministers are open to the idea of using other clergy in the ceremony, this is not always the case. In fact, some churches will not allow it. Therefore, you should check with the church before contacting any outside clergyman.

If a relative is a minister (perhaps a father or an uncle), asking him to give the charge to the couple or to open in prayer is a nice way to involve him in the ceremony.

PREMARITAL COUNSELING: A MODEL

It has been said that although God originated the institution of marriage, he gives us our marriages in kits; we have to assemble them here on earth. That is the purpose of premarital counseling—to teach you and your groom how to read the kit's instructions.

Each church handles premarital counseling differently. Pastors of small churches will probably offer individual counseling to couples. Larger churches, however, may offer this counseling to groups of engaged couples. Either method can be effective if it is done well.

If one of you is not available for several weeks before the ceremony, special arrangements will need to be made with the minister.

College Church of Wheaton, Illinois, has a particularly effective premarital counseling class covering many aspects of marriage, from communication to finances. One member of the pastoral staff leads these sessions through the structured curriculum outlined below.

The class meets on five consecutive Monday nights for approximately two hours of instruction and interaction each night. Everyone in the class is required to attend all five sessions and complete all homework assignments. Approximately two hours of "homework" are assigned for each session. Class members are asked to read three books of their choice on marriage and turn in summaries of what they have read and learned from each book.

Topics Discussed at the Premarital Class

1. Needs Assessment and Goal Formation. Each person coming into marriage has certain needs he or she believes the other person should fulfill. This class session attempts to identify these needs and expectations and help the couple verbalize them to each other. Likewise, the couple is encouraged to establish four long-range goals and four short-range goals for their marriage. They are then asked to select one of the specific goals and map out a plan for meeting that goal together.

2. Communication and Conflict Management. The basic ingredient for a healthy marriage is communication between the individuals. This session attempts to identify communication characteristics and encourage the couple to continually work on their communication skills.

Recognizing that every marriage is going to have conflicts, several different conflict-management styles are discussed.

3. The Biblical Basis for Christian Marriage. God has communicated to us through the Bible, and as Christians we need to know what the Bible says about marriage. This section of counseling deals with areas such as what a Christian marriage is, biblical submission, and the role of the man and woman in the context of marriage.

4. Sexuality and In-Laws. The first half of this session is taught by a gynecologist who provides information on the Christian view of sex and contraception. A detailed medical explanation is provided concerning human reproduction and modes of contraception. The counselees usually find this one of the most informative sessions.

The second half of the session deals with relationships with in-laws.

5. Finances and Family Relationships. This session of family finances is handled by a local Christian banker. The couple fills out a personal finance form, and the banker evaluates it in detail in light of present principles of finance, making suggestions he feels would be helpful.

The last half of the class deals with family relationships and such areas as children, names of children, relationships to the extended family, and certain myths about the American family.

The five sessions are taught by a variety of methods, including lectures, discussions, and interaction between members. Great emphasis is placed upon the desire to open communication channels and encourage the couples to talk about areas that might not otherwise be dealt with.

**Taylor-Johnson
Temperament Analysis Test**

Besides the five sessions, each couple is asked to take the Taylor-Johnson Temperament Analysis Test (TJTA) before they attend the initial premarital session.

The Taylor-Johnson Temperament Analysis Test is a revision of the Johnson Temperament Analysis, developed by Roswell H. Johnson and originally published in 1941. The text was revised and restandardized by Roger M. Taylor in 1967.

To administer the Taylor-Johnson Temperament Analysis Test the counselor or pastor must be certified. Often universities and colleges will offer the eight-hour certification course. Otherwise, the pastor can become certified through a one-day, eight-hour course, "The Christian Marriage Enrichment Taylor-Johnson Seminar." Once certified, he can send for the TJTA Manual and other necessary forms from Psychological Publications,

Incorporated, 5300 Hollywood Boulevard, Los Angeles, CA 90027. Psychological Publications will not send the necessary material until the certification process has been completed.

The test is intended to serve as a quick and convenient method of measuring nine areas of a person's temperament. It is designed primarily to provide visible evaluation, showing a person's feelings about him/herself at the time he/she answers the questions. The test is not designed to measure serious abnormalities or disturbances, but is extremely helpful in providing information to the counselor and counselees. The test is first taken by each individual to reveal how he/she perceives him/herself. The counselee is then asked to take the same questionnaire on his/her perception of his/her fiancé.

After scoring the tests, the counselor has five graphs used in counseling the engaged couple. Two graphs are of the individual returns. The third graph is an overlay of the individual returns. The fourth and fifth graphs, known as the "criss-cross," show how the individuals perceive themselves, and how their fiancés perceive them. The graphs are extremely useful in illustrating misconceptions about each other, areas where the couple's relationship is extremely strong, and areas where it is weak.

The engaged couples are scheduled to meet with the counselor for an hour and fifteen minutes to go over results of the TJTA on an individual basis. In this individual counseling session, they also complete the Premarital Communication Inventory (by Millard Biendenu, PhD, Counseling and Self-Improvement Programs, 710 Watson Drive, Natchitoches, LA, 71457).

This individualized session provides opportunity for the couple to ask the counselor personal questions. The counselor also has the opportunity to give homework and offer specific counsel to the couple. If a follow-up session is necessary, it is scheduled at this time.

In a premarital counseling session, the test is extremely valuable, because it provides graphic portrayals of the individuals entering the marriage and the couple that will soon be formed as man and wife. It slices through some people's facades and gets to the basic issues in their personalities.

HOW TO DESIGN A DO-IT-YOURSELF COURSE ON COUNSELING

If your church does not provide a counseling program, you may want to follow this procedure:

Locate an organization in your area which administers the TJTA. Schedule to have yourselves tested, and then meet with the counselor to go over the results.

Next, go to a Christian bookstore and find a recommended book on marriage. Purchase two copies of the book and work through the individual chapters together. One of the best books in the field is *A Handbook for Engaged Couples*, by Robert and Alice Fryling (InterVarsity Press, 1979). This workbook provides a structured format to allow you to deal with topics such as communication in marriage, problem solving, basic decisions, money, time, moods and emotions, the wedding, the honeymoon, and sex in marriage. Also, at the end of each chapter, there is a suggested reading which will allow you to look more deeply into some areas in which you may need to spend more time.

Major Decisions

When planning a wedding, one decision seems to depend upon another. The predetermined decisions give a basis for the others that need to be made.

If you have taken time to think things through, decide on a budget, and meet with your minister, you can now make some specific decisions, such as the date and time, the formality of the wedding, who your attendants will be, the reception site, the size of the guest list, your wedding dress, and the color scheme of the wedding.

DATE AND TIME

Many decisions will be easier to make once the date and time of the wedding are established.

Date. Certain dates are more popular than others for weddings. The months of June, August, September, and December, and holidays (such as Christmas and Thanksgiving) are regarded as excellent dates because of the extra vacation days that most people have. However, receptions are usually not well attended when held during a vacation month or on a weekday. (Exceptions to this are the evening reception and the Christmastime reception.)

Time. If your ceremony is to be held in the daytime, expect the attendance to be slightly lower because of guests who may have to work. You can safely expect about one-half to two-thirds of your invited guests to attend. (The wedding of a prominent person is usually attended by approximately 85 percent of the invited guests.)

An informal wedding is usually held during the day and can begin at whatever time you feel is convenient. If you live in the South or the West, you may need to consider the heat when determining the time of day. Often the custom of a particular group or church is a valuable guide to follow in determining the time.

The time of day your wedding is held will also affect what refreshments to serve at the reception. For instance, only light refreshments are necessary for weddings held between 2:00 P.M. and 3:30 P.M. or at 8:00 P.M. On the other hand, a sit-down meal is considered fashionable for formal weddings held at 12:00 or 12:30 P.M. or from 4:00 to 5:00 P.M.

FORMALITY OF THE WEDDING

Whether it be an ultraformal wedding with the reception held at an elegant ho-

31

tel, or an informal wedding in the bride's home with a buffet reception for family only, everyone has a different idea of a "dream" wedding. Today, most weddings are formal or semiformal. That is the style with which most people feel comfortable; they depart from strict etiquette a bit only for the sake of convenience or out of necessity. But you may prefer more formality or a homey atmosphere. Following are brief summaries of what the different formalities of a wedding entail.

The *ultra- or very formal* wedding means that you wish to follow strictly the traditional etiquette books. There will be a consistent style to your plans. This calls for a large guest list of over two hundred people, with the invitations, enclosures, and announcements engraved. The wedding should be held in a church or a large elegant room, and the reception should be equally luxurious—a sit-down meal amid an abundance of flowers and a musical background.

The bride of an ultraformal wedding will have a formal dress with a long train and a veil, with or without a blush veil. There may be from six to twelve bridesmaids with long formal dresses and bouquets, and possibly children attendants—junior bridesmaids, flower girls, train bearers, and a ring bearer. The groom will be dressed in a cutaway tuxedo.

The ushers and fathers should be dressed with the same propriety. The mothers' dresses will be floor length and made of fine fabric. The guests are expected to dress accordingly, although the women are not necessarily required to wear floor-length dresses.

It is best to have one usher for every twenty-five to fifty people.

You will know if your budget is in keeping with this style of wedding. If it is, your wedding will be a memorable experience for everyone involved.

The *formal wedding* is an extremely good choice, for practicality's sake. All the details can be scaled down from the ultraformal affair. The invitations may be printed or thermographed; the fathers may wear black dinner suits if they wish; the popular buffet-type reception, whether it be as a meal or light refreshment, is very satisfying. The guests need not feel pressured to dress in one particular fashion.

There may be less than two hundred guests, with one usher for every fifty people. As the bride, you may wear a long dress with a train and veil, and have from two to six bridesmaids.

A formal wedding is in no way an inexpensive affair, but it may be done with simplicity and good taste. It can have a tone of warmth that is sometimes lost in a more elaborate wedding.

A *semiformal wedding* has many of the same elements as the formal wedding. You have a choice of wearing a long gown or a street-length dress or suit, and may or may not decide to wear a headpiece. You may have one or two attendants, and usually up to one hundred guests attend.

An *informal wedding* can be a very relaxed affair with the ceremony taking place in a church or in a less formal setting. The invitations may be handwritten. As the bride, you may choose a street-length dress; the groom, as well as the best man, may be attired in a suit. You could have one attendant, and either carry bouquets or wear corsages. The reception of an informal wedding is usually a small, intimate one in a home or restaurant.

Whatever the style of your wedding, no one expects you to overextend yourself.

Yet, you will want to spend a great deal of effort making sure your special day is just right. Let the ceremony reflect all the love and regard you have for each other and for your guests.

CHOOSING YOUR ATTENDANTS
By this stage of planning, several dear friends have come to your mind. You no doubt want to honor all of them by asking them to be in your wedding, but that's not possible. Whom should you ask? Will you have to choose between your close child-hood friend or the warm, steadfast friend from work? How will you get around hurt-ing your college roommate who asked you to be in her wedding, if you decide not to ask her to be a part of yours?

The decisions made at this time are open to potentially adverse repercussions if not handled with great care and much thought. The best advice we can offer is to consider your family first. The months before a wedding, family ties are notice-ably strong and can be further strength-ened as a result of your decisions. Unless you are completely alienated from your brothers and sisters, you will find that they are the ones who usually will remain faithful to you through the years and who will continue to be the most interest-ed in your life. You will find a certain satisfaction in including them, and cer-tainly your friends will understand if you give preference to your siblings. I know one considerate bride who preferred to have sisters and even cousins attend her rather than choose between friends.

Some of your friends will be honored if you ask them to handle other duties such as attending the guest book or aiding with the reception tables. Cutting the cake is a difficult job, so a novice should

not be asked to do this.

If you *are* choosing friends, think of those who will take their responsibilities seriously enough to be of real help on that day. Also consider if these particular friends will mind the added expense of transportation (if they are from out of town), buying a gown that will usually be worn once, or renting the wedding attire. (Traditionally, the attendants pay for their own attire.) Spouses or fiancés of attendants should be included in the re-hearsal dinner also, and it would be a nice gesture to treat out-of-town attendants to breakfast the morning after the wedding.

RECEPTION SITE
Moving from the wedding to the recep-tion need not destroy the mood that the wedding has inspired, if the location and timing are kept in mind.

Church Reception
If your church has an area for a reception and is large enough for the number of guests you have decided on, it would make sense to have it there. It would be an ideal location, providing the facilities are equal to the reception you desire. If the room is less than the beautiful hall you were hoping for, don't let that bother you. This will hardly catch your guests' attention. There will be other things go-ing on that will—the aroma of fresh cof-fee, the sight of the beautiful wedding cake, the background music, and the com-pany of other friends. Gracious hospital-ity doesn't need an elaborate setting. If your goal is to make everyone feel spe-cial, then all who are there will have an outstanding time.

Before making your decision, deter-mine the following:

- Does the church have a reception committee that will handle the refreshments and services needed? or
- Will you need to hire a caterer or professional cook?
- Do you have friends who can help plan and carry out the reception?
- Is the kitchen equipment adequate? (For a full meal or just light refreshments?)
- Exactly what facilities are provided, and what are the fees involved?
- What is the guest limit according to the fire laws?
- What are the church's policies regarding decorations?

If you would really like to use the reception area in the church because of its convenience, but find that for some reason it is not ideal, consider these suggestions:

Too Small	Limit the number of guests invited to the reception.
	Simplify refreshments.
	Have a summer wedding so that doors may be opened to the outside if weather permits.
	Have half as many chairs as guests, giving more room for people to move around.
Too Large	Create a garden effect with rented or borrowed folding lawn furniture in one area.
	Block off a small area with roping or potted plants.
	Use small tables and lamps and oval rugs for conversation groupings.
	Put a fountain in the center.
Too Cold	Use space heaters.
Too Warm	Use fans if air-conditioning is unavailable.
Acoustics	Rent a sound system.
	Use a mobile amplification system.
Lighting	To change the mood, shut off some of the lights and substitute candles, hurricane lamps, or even living-room lamps.
	Arrange greens at the windows to diffuse the sunlight.
	Use battery-powered candles.
Electrical Outlets	If there are not enough, arrange for extension cords and check on load limit. (Be sure that cords are taped securely to the floor.)

If you do decide to go with the church reception facilities, ask to reserve them the day of the wedding, and perhaps the day before for any decorating you might like to do.

Hotel, Restaurant, or Private Club Reception

It is good to begin planning your reception as soon as possible after the date has been set. Some popular places are booked a year in advance. Consult friends for recommendations, or search the Yellow Pages and the newspapers for suggestions. Your church may even have a resource list of nearby places that have been satisfactory.

After you have compiled a list, call the reception sites and speak with the persons in charge of wedding receptions. Ask any questions you may have regarding the deposit, payment, and policies about a guarantee. Some require a deposit immediately to reserve a date. Others will allow you to reserve the date for a given amount of time before it has to be confirmed, but at that time a deposit will be required. In case of cancellation, the deposit is usually refunded only if the room is engaged by someone else, or the deposit can be applied to another party at another time.

The restaurant or hotel will ask for the approximate number of guests, and will suggest the room or rooms that are available. If there is a choice of rooms, ask which are the most desirable (take into account windows, if decorations are allowed, etc.). They are usually priced accordingly.

Ask about a reception "package," and what it includes—food and service only, or food and service with cake, decorations, music, etc. Ask to have any menus and other important information mailed to you so that you may compare and discuss the different alternatives at home.

RECEPTION SITE CHECKLIST	
TIMING	
What time segment does the fee cover? (Receptions usually last about three hours.)	
Will it be possible to decorate and prepare ahead of time? When?	
SPACE	
Where will the receiving line be formed?	
Is there space for throwing the bouquet (and the garter)?	
Where may the musicians perform?	
Is there ample space for chairs to be set up for elderly or invalid guests?	
FACILITIES	
Is there a piano? Is it kept in tune?	
Are coat racks out of sight?	
Are the chairs in good condition?	
Is there good china? Silverware? Tablecloths?	
Are there sufficient electrical outlets, refrigeration, cooking, and counter space?	
Who will set up tables? Who will clean up the area?	
Are there sufficient rest rooms? How far away are they?	

Make an appointment with the caterer or hostess at the reception facility that seems to meet your needs. You may want to go to several places. The caterer will show you the facilities and discuss the details with you. Get quotes of exact cost per person and rental fees. Inquire about music, flowers, and tipping policies. When meeting with the hostess, you will need to know an approximate number of guests expected so that you can decide on the menu and seating arrangements. Also decide at this time on the color of the tablecloths. Ask for a floor plan showing the arrangement of tables, where the receiving line might be set up, etc.

Many banquet facilities require that a bar be set up. Or, a flat rate might be charged even if you don't have the bar. This is usually the case only if your reception consists of a full-course dinner in the evening, though. To avoid the extra charge, consider having a late morning wedding. A brunch, luncheon buffet, or sit-down noon meal usually does not entail the bar charge.

When you call the week before the wedding with the definite number of guests attending, it would be wise to double-check all the details again.

Garden Reception

Certainly nothing could be more romantic or elegant than to have your reception on the lawn of a beautiful home. A tent should be provided for shade or in case of inclement weather, unless other shelter is available.

If you are thinking in this direction, take into account the expense of manicuring the lawn and garden, and providing the necessary catering services and equipment. Preparations need to be made days in advance if it is a formal affair.

The tent should be decorated with plants and flowers, and small tables should be set up for the guests, along with serving tables.

If you decide to do the reception totally on your own without the help of a caterer (see chapter 22), you will need to make arrangements for several items: the tent or canopy, tables and chairs, linen, china, flat silver, serving dishes, trays, candle holders, punch cups, ladles and bowls, and tea and coffee service.

You will also need to arrange for the services of a baker and the disposal of waste.

Consideration should be made for any musicians you may have. Find out if they will need special facilities.

These arrangements are for a formal reception. An informal reception can be scaled down to whatever you wish it to be, and can be quite successful if the weather permits.

Your New Apartment

If you are really daring, you may try to have a small reception at your new residence for a few special friends and relatives. A local delicatessen can provide anything from a roast turkey to fancy sandwiches. There are still the usual details that any reception must have: cake, punch, punch bowl, ladle, punch cups, plates, forks, tablecloths, napkins, flowers, etc. Just remember to have someone ready to clean this all up after you have left on your honeymoon or you will return to quite a mess!

GUEST LIST

One of the more challenging moments in your wedding preparation is deciding on the guest list. It *can* be an enjoyable time if you approach it in the right way.

Four different elements must be thought of when making up the guest list:

1. How many guests can you realistically invite?

If your ceremony location and budget allow for an unlimited number of guests, you will want to make sure not to forget anyone when sending out the invitations. Check address books, church directories, year books, and any other lists of names that you have, so as not to forget someone who is important to you.

On the other hand, your budget may end up determining how many guests you invite. One way to figure this out is to try to estimate the cost per person for the reception. It would be wise to set a limit for the number of guests, and then stick to that number. But hold a few places open on your list for any afterthoughts or unusual circumstances.

2. How shall the number be divided?

The decided number of guests may be divided in half, with one-half for your family and the other half for the groom's family. If one of the families lives quite a distance away, they may graciously concede part of their number.

Dividing the guest list into thirds is another practical way, with each set of parents having a third, and you and your groom having a third to invite your personal friends.

3. Who will you invite?

Begin your list with those you truly want to have with you on this memorable day, long-time friends or special people—those whose presence will be cherished. Include both of your families and grandparents, then move on to the bridal party (with their spouses and perhaps their parents), and close friends. If you have moved and have a new set of friends in a different part of the country from where you grew up (as is often the case nowadays), you may want to deemphasize the past in favor of the present.

Add to this those whom you are obligated to invite. A bridal party member may bring a fiancé, but it is not necessary for her to invite an escort. Parents of any children involved in the wedding should be invited, as well as your other relatives, the officiating clergy and spouse, anyone having hosted or served at a party given for you, any close friends of your parents or grandparents (if you know them), and neighbors (if they are in your circle of friends). Or, instead of sending them a wedding/reception invitation, consider inviting your neighbors over to the house after the wedding and reception for an informal buffet. This way they can still greet the bride and groom and feel a part of the festivities.

You may also consider inviting employers and co-workers to the wedding, but you are not obligated to do so. Inviting casual acquaintances or business associates is sometimes eyed with suspicion. This is not an occasion to be used to pay back social obligations or seek any type of political exposure.

Always remember: One member of a married couple is never invited without the other. And, even if the people on your "obligated" list don't come, at least you have done the courteous thing, and they will feel honored.

Out-of-town guests may or may not come to the celebration. If they do come, be prepared to give them the special attention they will need, such as housing, meals, and transportation.

You may find yourself forced to draw some lines. For instance, you may have to invite only those who live in the vicinity, and then send announcements to those living at a distance, or invite only the closest relatives and their families, leaving out the distant cousins. If the reception is to be a sit-down dinner, you may wish to invite adults only and provide baby-sitting for small children. When inviting people from a social group or the office, it is best to invite all or none of them so as to avoid any hurt feelings.

Send everyone on the list a wedding *and* reception invitation. Receiving a "wedding only" invitation is questionable, especially if others are receiving an invitation to both—although there are some exceptions to this:

- When the wedding is for the family only. A "reception only" invitation may be sent to the rest of your guest list.
- When you are planning a small reception located elsewhere. If you have certain people that you would like to have present at the wedding but can't invite to the reception, you may informally invite these people by contacting them personally. Directly after the wedding, you should have a receiving line at the church so these people may have a chance to wish you well. One idea might be to serve punch while the guests are greeted. In this way, everyone can leave with a sense of having participated in your happiness. Then, those with invitations may proceed to the reception.

4. *Are there any special circumstances?*

For instance, some brides choose to invite the entire membership of the church they attend, through a "blanket" invitation. In this case, no invitations would be sent except to relatives, very close friends, and those outside the church. An invitation can be read from the pulpit or printed in the bulletin on the Sunday before the wedding. This type of invitation may pose problems as you will probably not have a good idea of how many will actually come. Otherwise, invitations should be sent to *everyone* to avoid any hurt feelings.

After you, your mother, and your future mother-in-law have completed your lists, collate the two or three lists made, eliminating duplicate names. Be sure you get each person's full name and complete address (including zip code) from whoever is requesting this guest's presence. If you are going to send out announcements, this is a good time to compile a list for those, also.

Celebrate the completion of the final guest list by inviting your groom's mother to have lunch with you and your mother, if possible.

YOUR WEDDING DRESS

There is a thrill in staring into the three-way mirror and seeing yourself for the first time as a bride-to-be. Standing there in your wedding dress, you finally realize that the day you've worked and planned for will actually be a reality! More important than the fit or the train's length is whether the dress is especially suited to you. Every bride is a vision of loveliness, with a special beauty and glow. The wedding day and long after, you will be glad that you picked out the dress that was just right for you.

Your wedding dress will probably be the most expensive dress you will ever purchase. Your goal should be to have a beautiful dress that is comfortable and flattering to your figure . . . as well as your budget. It will be helpful to have an idea of the price range you can afford. Gowns are usually priced anywhere from $150.00 into the thousands of dollars. Veils usually run $45.00 and up.

There are many different styles of wedding dresses to choose from. Beginning with the natural waistline, a bouffant skirt or a straight skirt may be added. The shirtwaist may have a variety of skirts such as the A-line, gored, or bias. The princess style and empire waistline are perfect for a wedding gown as well.

Look through brides' magazines, getting a good picture in your mind of the type of dress you would like. Take note of the neckline, sleeves, waistline, fabric, and trimming. You will want a dress that will be attractive in your photographs as you look at them in the years to come.

White is the traditional color for the wedding dress, and it is the most appro-priate. There are many shades to take into consideration. Then there are the differing shades of ivory to consider, from deep cream to the antique tones. With the use of cosmetics, almost anybody can wear some shade of white. A hint of pastel at the waist or somewhere on the gown can be lovely, too.

A variety of trains are available also. A cathedral train is four- to six-feet long and is designed to be the width of an aisle. This is for the most formal weddings. A chapel-length train of one to three feet is for the formal or semiformal wedding. A sweep train also may be worn at a semiformal wedding. Lastly, a floor-length dress (or a slight sweep train) may be worn at an informal wedding.

There are a variety of headpieces and veils to choose from. It is good to have a basic understanding of what styles look best on a certain shape of face or figure. Below is a chart that will help you select the right headpiece and veil for you.

HEADPIECE AND VEIL SELECTION

HAIR	HEADPIECE*
all hair lengths	mantilla with ½ lift
short hair, curls around face	Juliet cap on back of head
chin-length wavy and fluffy hair	half-hat with a bit of veil behind
long hair swept back around shoulders	picture hat
long and smooth hair pulled off (round) face	face framer
shoulder-length hair	wreath
hair pinned up or waves	derby or boater hat
OTHER FEATURES	
round face with glasses	pillbox or off face and long smooth veil
tall	brimmed hat or tiny cap
full figure	neat and snug with veil
long face	face framer or poufy veil

*(Foundation for headpieces is buckram or horsehair cap covered with fabric, lace, flowers, etc.)

Traditionally, a cathedral-length veil (one foot or more on the floor), with or without a blush veil, is worn only with a gown that has a long train. This is seen at very formal weddings. A small hat that has a short veil covering only the eyes is considered informal. However, any of the following lengths is acceptable for a formal or semiformal wedding: shoulder, elbow, fingertip, and chapel or floor length (with or without a blush veil).

If a blush veil is used, it should not extend below the bride's bouquet.

It is also helpful to know that several types of veil fabrics are available, such as illusion, point d'esprit, and Russian net. Ask to see samples of these at a bridal shop or fabric store.

Making Your Own
No one will deny that a dress made by you or your mother adds a personal touch to your wedding. If you are making your own dress and veil, be sure you allow enough time. Shopping for a pattern and materials, fitting and sewing, and then refitting at the last minute if you happen to lose or gain any weight, all need to be taken into consideration.

Before buying a pattern, consider the style of clothing you usually wear. Perhaps you should go to a department store and try on the gowns or formals to get a better idea of what style looks best on you. Also, consider your hair style and the way you plan to wear it that day.

If you know someone who has a dress form in her attic, it might be helpful to borrow it, adjusting it to your size. Then you can drape your fabric on it in the way the pattern calls for, thus giving you a better idea of how your dress will turn out.

A word about laces and fabrics here will prove not only informative, but helpful.

Lace
A traditional wedding gown will have at least a touch of lace. It is the delicate lace together with the elegant fabric that gives the dress its special charm. Many of the laces that are used are imported.

The art of lacemaking started in Venice, Italy, and was encouraged in France. *Venice lace*, the most valuable of lace antiques, has a heavy appearance and is made of linen or cotton in leaf or floral patterns. It is usually white and is used as trimming on fine fabrics.

Another rare and valuable lace is *Chantilly*, from France. It is weblike in texture.

Alencon lace is from France as well. It is usually appliqued on fabric or used to embroider borders or hems. It is characterized by a floral or paisley pattern outlined with white thread that stands out called *cordonnet*. The pattern is connected by a net background.

Brussels lace, from Belgium, is delicate and lightweight with subtle configurations of pattern. It is limited in availability.

Nottingham, England, is famous for its laces and nets, hence the name *"English net."*

Most lace used now is machine-made of cotton thread. Almost every kind of lace made by hand can be duplicated accurately by machine.

Fabric
Whether or not you are planning on making your dress, you should be aware of the different fabrics wedding dresses can be made of. Most of the fabrics can be used for any degree of formality, as well

as any season. What you need to watch for is the weight of the fabric.

Some synthetics are wrinkle-free and may be worn all year round. Some silk fabrics are imported and are very delicate in texture, such as silk organza. Taffeta has proven to be a favorite. Or, a combination of fabrics is often used. Determine what you'd like and then shop around for the best prices.

When you do purchase your dress fabric, make sure your veiling matches it. (It may be difficult to determine the exact color of the fabric under commercial lighting.) Some fabric shops have booklets on making your own veils which are of great assistance. Also at this time, purchase the buckram or horsehair cap for your headpiece. (You might want to buy extra fabric to cover it.)

Other Alternatives
Perhaps the idea of making your own wedding dress does not appeal to you. Well, there are several other options. Possibly your family, your groom's family, or a friend has an heirloom gown you can wear. (Although borrowing from a friend can be touchy, since the gown can be damaged accidentally.) Your mother's gown may be waiting for you, and you may want to wear it either for sentimental or economic reasons. If that is the case, you should have it custom fit to your figure. But a word of caution: Cleaning and restoring a used gown can be a very difficult process, and is usually not guaranteed. Therefore, your mother will probably understand if you decline in favor of having your own dress.

Renting a gown is seldom done anymore.

The most obvious alternative, of course, is purchasing a new dress. Department stores have experienced consultants to help you. Their selection may be more limited, but they are willing to help with all your needs. Even if you know you will not be purchasing one of their gowns, it might still be helpful to attend one of their bridal shows to see the latest fashions. Or, if you are a size ten or smaller, you may be able to get a deal on a display dress; there are often sales on manufacturers' samples.

Bridal showrooms often have substantial discounts on their gowns. They have all the accessories, as well as a bridal consultant at your service. However, they usually do not do fitting or altering, and you must arrange for pick up and final pressing.

You could have your dress made to order for you by a designer or dressmaker. This way you can be sure that it will be originally created for you. A designer's staff of seamstresses is ready to please you. Many of the current designers have a line of wedding attire already created (e.g., Laura Ashley), which you can try on in their shops or at local department stores.

Take your mother or a good friend along when you try on dresses. Their objective thoughts will be helpful. Other things to take along would be a pair of shoes similar in height to the ones you will wear with the dress, and the bra you will most likely wear that day. It is also wise to fix your hair and makeup so they will be similar to how they will be the day of the wedding. Take anything that needs to be matched with the dress, such as an heirloom veil. This way you will get a good idea of how you will look and feel on the actual wedding day.

Because their focus is mainly on weddings, bridal shops are equipped to give you excellent service. When someone recommends a particular one to you, this is a good sign that *you* will probably be pleased as well. A former bride's mother will be quick to tell you if she did not receive good service.

Your consultant at a bridal shop will be able to advise you on appropriate fabrics for the season of your wedding, and the color that is the most flattering on you. She will ask if you have decided on a particular style and from that and other guidelines you offer, she will be able to show you some dresses. Some shops will let you browse through their sample inventory as well. However, there is no substitute for trying the dresses on. You will be able to tell by looking in the mirror which dress is just right for you. If you're apprehensive about making a mistake, *take your time.* The more you look, the more you'll learn, and the more certain you will be when you find the *right* dress for you!

Plan to order your dress six months in advance, if possible. The consultant will take your measurements while you are in the shop so she can order the dress accordingly. At most bridal shops, hem alterations are usually included in the price, while other alterations will probably be extra. If you are tall, you will need to order extra length.

When the dress arrives ten to twelve weeks later, you will be asked to come to the shop for your first fitting. Any adjustments will take an additional two to four weeks. The last alterations should be only a few days before the wedding so you can be sure of a perfect fit.

Here are some pointers to keep in mind when being fitted: The bust line should fit smoothly, with the darts in line with the fullest part of the bust. The sleeves should have some fullness for easy movement. If the sleeves are long, they should touch the wrist bone when your elbow is bent; any lace on the end of the sleeve should fall over the hand. If the lace comes to a point, the point should be in line with the ring finger. The dress length should be 1½ to 2 inches from the floor and the dress should hang evenly all around when the train is bustled up in the back.

It is possible to rush all the steps involved in purchasing your dress, if necessary. But keep in mind that spring is always the busiest time of the year, so be prepared to find that a store may not be able to accommodate you then if you wait very long to place your order.

Here are some questions you may want to ask when shopping for a dress:

- Can you order a certain dress you saw pictured in a magazine?
- Can the manufacturer make major changes in the neckline, sleeves, etc.?
- What are the shop's policies on alterations and fittings?
- What are their payment arrangements? (Get this information in writing.)
- Do they deliver, or is the dress packed in tissue to be carried in your car?
- What are the pressing instructions?
- Will they provide extra fabric so you may cover your headpiece (if you need this done)?
- How many days before the wedding will the last fitting be done?
- Does the shop happen to give any discounts on flowers, photographs, etc.?
- Will one of their staff come to help you get into the dress on the day of your wedding?

COLOR SCHEME

A particular fabric or dress design that you'd like for the bridesmaids undoubtedly comes in a choice of colors. When selecting a color, it is best to keep in mind the decor of the church, if that's where you're getting married. If your ceremony is to be held at home, take careful note of the pattern of the draperies and furniture, so that a harmonious effect may be achieved.

Also consider the particular flowers which will be in season. For instance, yellows and pastels in the spring, roses and blue flowers in the summer, and bronzes and mauves in the fall. Of course, Christ-

---

WEDDING DRESS ACCESSORIES

Gloves. Wrist-length lace gloves are becoming more and more popular. Traditionally, though, the bride wears long gloves of kid (lined with silk), lace, or a fabric that matches, with an elbow-length sleeve or sleeveless dress. Lace gauntlets might be worn with a long-sleeved dress. They are, however, optional and would be inappropriate for a home wedding.

Gloves are optional for a semiformal and informal wedding as well. If gloves are worn by the bride, the inseam of the ring finger on the left hand will need to be unstitched so that the glove may be slipped off the finger and the ring may be slipped on.

Shoes. Ballet slippers have become very popular with brides because they are comfortable for standing in the receiving line. They are also a good choice if the groom is not very tall. They come in white satin and may be dyed.

A little lift will give a better contour to the body, however, so if it is possible, choose a fabric shoe that may be dyed to match the gown. A pump is most appropriate, but a sandal is often worn.

Hosiery. Choose a pale color or possibly white.

Lingerie. Pale nude is the best under white.
You may need a special bra or a waist nipper.
Wedding dresses usually have linings, but a slip may be recommended. (Remember that it is bound to show when you lift your dress to go up to the platform.)
Crinoline is better than a hoop for an old-fashioned dress.

Other. A small handbag matching the shoes or dress in which to carry touch-up makeup.
A minimum of jewelry. You might want to wear a gift from the groom if it is appropriate. Carrying a handkerchief is a nice thought, too, if you can manage it with your bouquet.
Traditionally you will want to remember something old, something new, something borrowed, and something blue!

mas means lots of green and red in all shades.

The complexion of the attendants should be taken into consideration as well. If most of your party looks washed out in shades of yellow, then it would be best to avoid that color. Almost anyone is beautiful in one of the many shades of blue that are available. Blue tends to be very flattering on mothers as well. White isn't a bad color to think about, either, but care needs to be taken that makeup is used to heighten natural skin tone.

Well, with all of the decisions that you've made as you've worked through this chapter, you are well on your way to having a perfectly beautiful wedding! So now let's make plans to capture it in pictures. . . .

BRIDE'S WEDDING ATTIRE CHECKLIST		
	Cost	
	ESTIMATED	ACTUAL
Wedding Gown	$ _____	_____
Veil	_____	_____
Headdress	_____	_____
Accessories		
Shoes	_____	_____
Hosiery	_____	_____
Lingerie	_____	_____
Other (gloves, jewelry, etc.)	_____	_____
Fitting dates	_____	
Final date	_____	
Pick up	_____	
Total	$ _____	_____

CHAPTER SEVEN

Photography

A wooden frame bordering a heart-shaped sepia-colored photograph hangs on the wall in my family room. It has captured a poignant moment as a bride and groom, surrounded by friends, leave the church after the wedding.

One touching, nostalgic shot can conjure up all the excitement you experienced at your wedding as you and your groom look back through your pictures in the years to come. The wedding day will be more memorable if the events of the day are recorded by a reliable photographer.

When looking for a photographer, be sensitive to his artistry if you want him to capture the tone of the wedding. Don't let the fade-outs and superimposed shots convince you of his creativity; these are routine. He will need to be perceptive in order to see what others may miss. Candid shots of children, grandparents, and other guests, as well as of the two of you, will bring back memories long after the formally posed pictures are put away. You will relive your wedding day many times, and it is a mistake to think you will remember the details.

All around you cameras will start clicking the moment you announce your engagement. The bridal shower, other parties, and the rehearsal dinner are all good picture-taking moments. For these special events you may want to provide someone with a camera and film to be sure you'll get some pictures for your scrapbook.

If you ask a friend to take your wedding pictures, be sure your friend is reliable and has had some experience doing weddings. It is difficult for a friend to work at a wedding and to enjoy it as well. It may be better to ask your friend to take some of the shots, but still have a professional handle the majority of the responsibility. There have been many sad and disappointing stories resulting from well-meaning friends who could not really handle the job.

SELECTING A PHOTOGRAPHER

Consider the most reputable and experienced photographers in the area. Ideally, a professional photographer should have a reputation for a mannerly approach, catching the mood of the occasion, providing excellent proofs, and producing a beautiful album. The importance of an excellent photographer should not be underestimated.

Ask to see friends' wedding albums.

Check for these details: Do the subjects look relaxed and natural, or unexpressive and stiff? Do you like the style? Do the candids portray interesting incidents, or are they dull? Ask your friends about the photographer's technique, his professional conduct, and his promptness.

Then phone several photographers to compare costs, services, and availability. Prices do vary from one to another, based on status, location, and time needed. Find a photographer who can work within your time schedule. Ask about his "package" and what is included. You may even ask for references if you feel this is necessary. Photographers expect this type of interview, so feel free to do the asking.

Engage someone who will take the kind of pictures you want. Some specialize in portraits only, while others specialize in the entire wedding proceedings. If you prefer to have twenty-five quality portraits rather than hundreds of candid shots, then choose your photographer accordingly. It is good if he is a member of the Professional Photographers' Association of America, which has its own code of ethics for wedding photography. However, this does not determine his skill.

Consultations

When you have made your choice, make an appointment for a consultation. When you meet with the photographer:

1. Look at samples again. If you like a certain set of pictures, make sure to get that particular photographer, not his assistant.
2. Discuss the bridal portrait. (See the section in this chapter labeled "The Bridal Portrait.")
3. Discuss informal and candid pictures. Have a clear understanding of what

you are getting for your money. Give the photographer a list of people you definitely want photographed—both formal and candid. This way he can be prepared.
4. Get prices on various sizes of prints. The standard sizes are 8″ x 10″, 5″ x 7″, 3½″ x 5″. You may order them larger or get wallet sizes if you wish. Make sure to ask him how long he will keep the negatives after the wedding.
5. Plan the order in which he will take the pictures. You'll also want to know the exact time he will be at each location. Some parts of the ceremony can be acted out beforehand in order to get close-up shots.

If you plan to have pictures taken before the wedding, including the bridal portrait at the church, you will need to be at the church about three hours before the wedding. This allows forty-five minutes to dress, one to one and a half hours for photographs, and forty-five minutes for the sanctuary to be clear before the wedding so the guests may be seated. Everyone does not have to be there at the same time during the photographs. It's nice if formals with the families are scheduled closest to the wedding so that family members don't have to come as early and wait as long.
6. Give him a copy of the church's policies for weddings. This way he can know such do's and don'ts as:

• No flashbulbs or altar photography during the ceremony.
• Must remain unobtrusive. (If you want pictures taken during the actual ceremony, have your photogra-

pher do this with time exposure from the back of the sanctuary. This will prevent any distractions.)

- Never be between guests and the ceremony.
- Wear a dark suit and a name badge for identification.

7. Discuss final prices. The photographer will usually have a "package" with a certain number of pictures at a given price. This is not always realistic, because you may want more prints. Ask if the price includes an album. Also ask if his transportation is included in his fee. Often a photographer will request a meal if his service runs over five hours.

8. Make a firm financial arrangement. A written confirmation or contract should include such things as the number of photographs you are obliged to buy, the delivery date of proofs and finished prints, who owns the negatives, liability if originals are lost, and what the payment arrangements are, from the deposit to the final payment.

9. Make arrangements for him to see the wedding site ahead of time. This way he can make arrangements for lighting and filter requirements.

10. Ask the photographer to give everyone with a camera an opportunity to take a particular shot before he takes the final one, such as leaving the church.

THE BRIDAL PORTRAIT

The bridal portrait is a lovely way to preserve the beauty and importance of the bride on a day set apart from the rest. Sometimes the bridal portrait is over-

looked because of inconvenience or cost. However, a portrait can be a nice display piece for your home, or it may be displayed by loving parents.

There are a number of places you could have it done. When selecting the place (and the final pose), keep in mind that the portrait should reflect the true nature of your wedding.

Each of the following would be good locations to have your portrait taken:

1. *The bridal salon or department store* where you have purchased your dress may have a suitable room. This would work out well because you wouldn't have to worry about transporting your dress and veil.

2. *The photographer's studio* has the most ideal lighting, background, and atmosphere. Your dress and veil will have to be packed and carried, or delivered there.

3. *At home.* You may desire some informal poses on a stairway or in the garden of your home. The photographer may also be able to provide a backdrop suitable for more formal poses there.

4. *The church before the ceremony.* Portrait-like shots are usually taken at the church, and may be very nice and much less expensive. You would then plan to dress early at the church.

   The advantages of this are that you will have your own bouquet and the realism of your wedding day will have dawned on you.

5. *Your photographer may have other suggestions.*

You may want to have your portrait taken as soon as you have the final fitting of your gown, as much as a month before the wedding (although most brides schedule their final fitting only a few days before the wedding). It would be good to have a time set aside when you feel relaxed and composed.

Think of your portrait as a dress rehearsal for the wedding. Style your hair and makeup as you will for the wedding. You will look your best if you are rested and have eaten a meal beforehand. Ask the photographer's advice on makeup. Most important, you'll want to accent your eyes with a touch of mascara, but it shouldn't be too heavy. Be natural—wear your hair in the style you usually wear it. Don't be too different. Clear nail polish is more pleasing with your formal wedding attire. Be careful not to overdo the jewelry; a simple strand of pearls or a gold chain is enough, perhaps with tiny pearls or gold balls for earrings. Take everything with you that you will wear on your wedding day.

Your photographer should take both full-length and head-and-shoulder poses. When the proofs arrive, you may want to order a 5″ x 7″ black and white glossy for the newspaper announcement. You may choose another pose to keep for yourself and/or to give to your parents.

Dressing Up for Your Bridal Portrait
Lingerie
- [ ] White or nude color
- [ ] Bra that you wore when you were fitted
- [ ] Panties
- [ ] Hosiery (ultrasheer flesh color)
- [ ] Slip or appropriate liner
- [ ] Foundation, if needed

Makeup if you use it (nothing heavy)
- [ ] Liquid or cream base
- [ ] Blush—Not too much!
- [ ] Lip gloss, medium shade

- [ ] Eye makeup—Mascara is needed for pictures
- [ ] Deodorant
- [ ] Nail polish for touching up manicured nails

Hair needs
- [ ] Some kind of curling iron or rollers for quick touch-up
- [ ] Comb and brush
- [ ] Hair spray—Spray a bit on your hand and touch up your hair
- [ ] Hair pins for headpiece
- [ ] Safety pins

Miscellaneous
- [ ] Wedding gown, pressed
- [ ] Wedding shoes
- [ ] Wedding jewelry, if any
- [ ] Headpiece and veil
- [ ] Gloves
- [ ] Possibly an iron for quick touch-ups
- [ ] Light snack

Remember something old, something new, something borrowed, something blue!

AT THE WEDDING
Remind the photographer a few days before the wedding exactly where he is to be and when he is to be there.

Give a duplicate list of pictures to be taken to a close friend or the wedding hostess. This person can assist the photographer in rounding up the people.

Most professional photographers will not allow anyone else to take flash pictures while they are working on the formal poses. If this is the case with your photographer, remind family and friends of this ahead of time.

Much of the wedding tension can be eliminated if all of the posed pictures are taken before the ceremony. But in order to preserve that special moment when your groom first sees you in your wedding dress, ask the minister or wedding hostess to arrange for a room off to one side where the two of you can meet alone for a few moments before proceeding with the pictures.

If you really do *not* want your groom to see you before you walk down the aisle, arrange for family pictures and separate formals to be taken beforehand. This will cut down considerably on the picture-taking time needed later.

If any pictures *are* to be taken after the ceremony, there must be a time limit set so as not to be rude to your waiting guests.

It's a good idea to supply cameras and film to someone from each of your families. These persons could be responsible for taking shots of people in their own family that might otherwise be missed. Or another fun idea is to have someone at the reception armed with a Polaroid instant camera and plenty of film. This person could take pictures that you could look through on your honeymoon, or, the guests could be presented with pictures of themselves.

OTHER PERMANENT RECORDINGS

Many churches have an audio system available for tape recording your ceremony. This is totally acceptable and causes little inconvenience, especially if the church owns a microphone that will simply clip on to the pastor's lapel. A microphone set up near you and the groom will not be distracting, either, though. It is actually desirable so that your guests may hear your exchange of vows.

If no audio system is available, a hidden cassette tape recorder *may* pick up the service adequately.

Videotaping can be done with good results if done with discretion by an expert. The camera should be modern with low light capabilities and a telephoto lens. The operator should be efficient and knowledgeable. Before hiring one, look at samples of his work to see if the editing suits your wishes.

For any of these methods of recording, you will need to give the operator information regarding what you expect, times and locations, and what length of tape you would like.

SAMPLE PHOTOGRAPHY CHECKLIST

Person	Time	Where	What	With whom
Bride			Portrait	Alone ✓
	Before ceremony		*Informals*	
			Adjusting veil	Mother ✓
			Dressed	Alone
				Father ✓
				Both Parents ✓
				Honor attendant ✓
				Maids together ✓
				With each
				1.
				2.
				3.
				4.
			Touching up makeup, hair, etc.	
			Leaving house	
			Getting into car	Father
			Arriving at church	
			Greeting	Groom's parents ✓
			Meeting groom	Groom ✓
		Church	*Posed*	Groom ✓
				Parents ✓
				Groom and honor attendants ✓
				Attendants ✓
				Groom and entire party ✓
				Groom and all parents
				Groom and his parents and family ✓
				Groom and bride's parents and family ✓
				Groom and other people
				1.
				2.
				3.
				Groom and flower girl and ring bearer
		Aisle	*More informals*	
			Processional	Father
			Meeting	Groom
			Ceremony	
		Church	Recessional	Groom
		Church steps		Alone
				Groom

SAMPLE PHOTOGRAPHY CHECKLIST (cont.)

Person	Time	Where	What	With whom
Bride			Receiving line	Groom, guests
			Reception-arriving	Groom
			Getting out of car	Groom
			Cutting cake	Groom ✓
			Feeding each other	Groom ✓
			Dining	Groom
			Throwing bouquet	Unmarrieds
			Garter removing	Groom
			Ready to leave	Groom ✓
			Saying good-bye	Groom and parents
				Flower girl
				School friends
				Groom and office friends
Groom			Leaving house	Alone
			Posed	Father
				Alone
				Parents
				Groomsmen ✓
				Best man
				Pastor and best man etc. (see bride's posed list)
			Throwing garter	Bachelors
Groomsmen			Getting bout.	
			Catching garter	
			Decorating car	
Bridesmaids			With escorts	
			Each alone	
			Catching bouquet	
			Decorating car	
Wedding party			Getting flowers	
Ring bearer			Posed	Alone
				With parents
Flower girl			Posed	Alone
				With parents
Musicians ✓				
Guest book ✓ attendant			Holding pen out to guest	Guest
Gift attendant			At gift table	
Friends serving ✓ punch				
1.				
2.				
3.				
4.				

SAMPLE PHOTOGRAPHY CHECKLIST (cont.)

Person	Time	Where	What	With whom
Personal attendant	_____	_____	Helping the bride	Bride
Wedding coordinator	_____	_____		
Bride's parents	_____	_____		Alone Table Guests
Groom's parents	_____	_____		Alone Table Guests

Guests
  Relatives
  1.
  2.
  3.
  4.
				Small informal groups
				Throwing rice
				Waving good-bye

Unmarried girls	_____	_____		Catching bouquet
Bouquet and garter catchers	_____	_____		Together

When you receive your proofs, try to go through them objectively. You can then begin to formulate a realistic pattern for a lovely album. If you line them up in chronological order, it will flow with some continuity.

ORDERING PHOTOGRAPHS

WHO ORDERS	WHAT	FOR WHOM	COST
Bride's parents	Bridal portrait	Themselves	_____
	Wedding album	Bride and groom	_____
	Extra prints	Themselves	_____
Bride and groom	Picture of each other for desk or dresser at home or at work	Each other	_____
	Bridal portrait	Themselves	_____
	Small portrait of bride	For parents	_____
	Album		_____
	Couple		
	Members of immediate family with newlyweds		
	Both sets of parents together		
	Receiving line		
	Parents' table		
	Small print of whole wedding party with bride and groom	Attendants	_____
	Individual print	Attendants	
Groom's parents	Should have opportunity of selecting from proofs if desired		_____
Favorite aunts or friends	May appreciate being able to select some special shots		_____

Flowers

Flowers add greatly to the beauty and grandeur of a wedding. An attractive display helps set the tone for the event as the guests arrive, as well as make a lasting impression after they leave.

You may have a friend or relative who is experienced and capable of handling the floral needs of your wedding. A great deal of expense can be avoided if this person agrees to arrange the flowers for you. You will be greatly indebted to him or her. To avoid problems, though, make sure this person has enough time to invest and understands exactly what you want.

On the other hand, the convenience of a good professional florist is immeasurable. Look for one with a good reputation for sensitivity to your desires, one who makes deliveries on time, and one who gives quality as well as quantity for your money.

The best way to locate a good florist is to get recommendations from former brides. Previous satisfaction is your best guide. The florist should be able to offer advice on the flowers suitable for the season and your budget, and suggest the appropriate shape and proportional size of the bouquets.

If he is familiar with your church or ceremony location, so much the better.

You should receive an itemized bill in advance. This should include the details

CONSULTING WITH THE FLORIST

- Know about how much you want to spend or your limit for floral needs.
- List the flowers you like best, also second choices.
- List floral needs and discuss:
  1. The roles of the colors of the dresses.
  2. The use of fresh flowers as opposed to silk flowers.
- Bring a sketch of the front and side views of your dress.
- Listen to the florist's suggestions— be open-minded about seasonal flowers.
- Agree on a color scheme.
- Discuss decorations for the sanctuary. Will he view the sanctuary and reception site?
- Discuss the delivery time and set-up duties. (A chart is useful for this with a duplicate copy given to the florist.)
- Discuss other items that may be supplied (candelabra, aisle runner, etc.).
- Ask for a cost estimate in writing.
- Check out the ribbons, doilies, and other accessories he might use. Does he use dyed flowers? Ask for a sample ahead of time.

you have agreed on, such as the delivery and set-up times, and locations.

Plan on your floral needs consuming 15 to 25 percent of your total budget.

FLOWERS FOR THE BRIDE

Several factors should be taken into consideration when ordering your bouquet. These include the formality of the wedding, as well as the texture and color of your dress. It would be advisable to bring a sketch of the front and side views, along with a description of the neckline and sleeve length when you meet with the florist. A swatch of fabric would also be helpful.

An attractive "cloud" bouquet gives a light, airy effect. A few flowers may be placed randomly in a cloud of smaller flowers (such as baby's breath) and finished with a bit of greenery. You may prefer the traditional white flowers with a background of greens or a touch of color to offset the white. A single unusual flower as a central focal point, which could be taken out later and saved, or worn as a corsage, is also an alternative. As the bride, you may want to include flowers in your bouquet that have a particular significance to you: Possibly the first flowers your groom ever gave you, or a flower that both your mother and your grandmother carried in their wedding bouquets. All of these things should be kept in mind when talking with your florist.

Other flowers to consider might include a headpiece to be worn alone or attached to the veil, a spray of flowers for the hair to be pinned in at the reception if the veil is removed, and a small bouquet to "throw away" in order to preserve the wedding bouquet. Or, in place of a veil, a very nice effect—especially if you have long hair—is to have flowers tied into lace ribbons that drape down the back from a crown of flowers.

If you are having an informal wedding, a corsage which complements your street-length suit or dress could be chosen instead of a bouquet.

It's a nice gesture on your wedding day to present each mother with a rose. You may carry these roses with your bouquet, or they may be placed in the chancel area to be given to the mothers before or after the ceremony.

Think about carrying a sprig of ivy with your flowers. The sentimental value of having something to grow from the wedding might add a bit of nostalgia to the years ahead.

THE BRIDESMAIDS' FLOWERS

These bouquets are chosen by the bride to harmonize with the style and color of the bridesmaids' dresses. They may be in matching or contrasting colors and be chosen from a variety of styles. Sometimes the honor attendant's bouquet will be of a slightly different color. Delicate silk or velvet flowers may be inserted into fresh flower bouquets or hairpieces, thereby enhancing your color scheme.

Care should be taken in considering the proportions of the bouquets to the bridesmaids and the church. Large bouquets will overwhelm or cover the dresses and are not in good taste. Bouquets that are too small will appear insignificant.

Bring a sketch of the bridesmaids' dresses and a swatch of their fabric with you when you meet with the florist.

A nice tradition is to place the bouquets around the cake or on the bridal table at the reception for effective table decorations.

Bouquets of silk flowers will make elegant table centerpieces or wall hangings and serve as mementos for years to come. Because of this, they are often given to the bridesmaids as gifts.

BOUTONNIERES

Boutonnieres are small flowers worn by the men in the wedding party, the fathers, the grandfathers, and any other man you wish to honor. Traditionally, they are white, but may be in a color harmonizing with the color scheme of the wedding. The style and color of the men's attire should be noted before ordering.

The groom's boutonniere should be different from the rest. It is usually a flower similar to one in your bouquet. You may also choose to have your groom go without a boutonniere until you join him at the altar. If you do this, you could then take a flower from your bouquet (which has previously been prepared) and pin it on his lapel at that time. Just be sure he has one when the pictures are taken.

The fathers' boutonnieres can be alike, and are usually some type of white flower. Simple white carnations may be provided for the ushers. Extra boutonnieres could be provided for the organist, soloist, musicians, helpers, hosts, and clergyman (if he doesn't wear a robe). It is also wise to order an extra boutonniere in the event that you have forgotten someone.

OTHER FLOWERS

Junior Bridesmaids' Bouquets
Miniature in size, they should match the bridesmaids' in style and color.
Flower Girl
May carry a miniature bouquet of tiny flowers or a small basket of flowers or rose petals to scatter before the bride.
Ring Bearer
You may want to get some extra flowers to place on the pillow that the ring bearer will carry.
Headpieces for Attendants
Style and length of hair should be considered. Small matching flowers in bandeau (headband), crown, or barrette are possibilities. Heavy flowers are not suitable.
Mothers' Corsages
They need not be exactly alike, but should be similar in design. They can be made of a special flower or flowers to blend with the colors worn. They may be pinned at the shoulder, waist, or on a purse, or you (or they) may desire that wrist corsages be worn. Glamelias (gladiolas that are taken apart, wired, and formed into a single flower) are a particularly nice flower for this. They are lightweight and may be made in a variety of colors.
Grandmothers' Corsages
They don't need to be exactly alike, and are usually done in pastel colors to coordinate with their dresses.

There is an endless list of people who could receive corsages if your budget lends to this. It is nice to remember people who are special to you. A single flower, neither large nor overpowering, is a nice thank you, but is not necessary. Some of these people include:
Soloists
Organist
Musicians
(If any of these charge a fee, then extra flowers are not necessary. Violinists usually do not wear corsages.)

Others:
  Guest book attendant
  Gift attendant
  Personal assistants
  Reception assistants:
    cake servers

hostess
hospitality committee
Sister, sister-in-law
Special helpers
Special people in your life
Wedding coordinator

BOUQUET IDEAS

BRIDE

Traditional cascade—flowers and ivy

T-shaped cascade

Round nosegay with a ribbon shower (may tie "love knots" [single knots not pulled tightly] at varying intervals in the ribbons)

Long-stemmed arm arrangement with ribbons

Basket

Single flower—rose, peony

Arrangement on a Bible—single or spray of small flowers with ribbons

Crescent

Cloud arrangement

Fan-shaped or on a fan

On a parasol

Flowers intertwined with roping for the waist or draped from shoulder to waist

Shoulder handbag with tiny flowers tucked in

Three long-stemmed roses, one to be given to each mother after the processional or before the recessional, and one to be kept by the bride

BRIDESMAIDS

Any of the above, or

Small baskets with ivy

Hat decorations

Wrist bouquets

White wicker baskets with flowers and ribbons

Hurricane lamps with holly wreaths

Heart-shaped wreaths

Bouquet pinned on a velvet muff

Parasol

Contemporary arrangement

Golden ornaments in pine

Variegated greenery

Glamelias

BOUQUET IDEAS (cont.)

FLOWERS OFTEN USED FOR THE BRIDE

Camellias
Gardenias
Lilies of the valley
Freesia
Baby's breath
Roses
Lilies
Orchids (white, cymbidium, phalaenopsis, cattleya)
White heather
Stephanotis
Pompons
Carnations
Gladiolas
Narcissus
Chinese Peonies
Zinnias
Cosmos
Asters
Hydrangea
Michaelmas daisies
Jasmine
Magnolias
Tulips
Irises
Pansies
Queen Anne's lace
Candytuft

Greens: Ivy, lemon leaves, ferns (springeri [asparagus], leatherleaf)

CHURCH FLOWERS

Many churches are architecturally beautiful, so it may be unnecessary to have a large display of flowers. Recent trends have been toward simplicity in the sanctuary decorations, so that emphasis can be placed on the worship service. Huge baskets of flowers are often replaced by a simple floral arrangement or arrangements of greens along with candles in the chancel area. Greenery is something to consider because it adds serenity to the dignity of the service. It can be draped along the baptistry, choir rails, and/or window ledges.

Potted plants are especially lovely if a more symmetrical arrangement is desired. They may sometimes be rented from a florist. The pots should be hidden if they are placed along railings or grouped about the stairs or candelabras. House plants often do not give the desired effect as they are usually too small. Potted plants tend to make the atmosphere more informal.

Small flowering plants in the windows could be attractive, also. Garlands of flowers and ribbons may be used on the pews. Topiary trees or tubs of geraniums on either side of the entrance to the church give a nice appearance. Archways and trellises are sometimes used. But caution needs to be taken with these—they are a great concern to those with full skirts, hats, and/or veils.

Keep in mind that flowers should be at eye level or above to be seen. Each church usually determines its own set of rules. Therefore, it is best to ask if there are regulations concerning the size of the flower arrangements, whether the florist is allowed to decorate the chancel area, and whether artificial or silk flowers may be used.

BUDGET AND BASIC FLORAL NEEDS

Ceremony site_____ Address _____ Person to see _____

Date _____ Time_____ Phone_____ Color scheme_____

| ITEM | FLORIST | | | | | | | |
	NUMBER	KIND	COLOR	EST. COST	ACT. COST	MAKE YOURSELF	EST. COST	ACT. COST
Church Decorations								
Chancel								
Aisles								
Windows								
Other								
Aisle runner								
Candles								
Candelabra								
Attendants								
Maid of Honor								
Bridesmaids								
Others								
Corsages								
Grandmothers								
Assistants								
Others								
Mothers' roses								

RECEPTION FLOWERS

The right balance of flowers is very important at the reception. They should not be overdone. Small, low centerpieces for the guests' tables and epergnes (ornamental containers that attach to the candelabras) with artistic floral arrangements around the candelabra on the head tables are beautiful. If a garden effect is desired, the entire hall can be transformed with trees, bushes, and wicker baskets with blooming plants. Hanging ferns and a gazebo might complete the picture.

If your wedding and reception are at home, arrange greens tastefully in the ceremony area. You might consider having a rope of greens, with flowers tucked in, strung from one bridesmaid to the next. They would stand evenly spaced, while you would walk down the aisle. Then the bridesmaids would gather up the rope and hold it in front of them (as a bouquet) as they take their places.

For a holiday wedding reception, an arrangement for each table might be a mirrored mat placed in the center with a squatty hurricane lamp and candle placed upon it. A wreath around the candle of fresh pine and golden balls completes this festive centerpiece.

BUDGET AND BASIC FLORAL NEEDS (cont.)

Reception site _____ Address_____ Phone_____

| | FLORIST | | PHONE | | | | | |
	NUMBER	KIND	COLOR	EST. COST	ACT. COST	MAKE YOURSELF	EST. COST	ACT. COST
Table centerpieces Bride's Parents' Guests' Other								
Other decorations Top of cake Around cake Cake knife Receiving line area Other			Total	$	$	Total	$	$
GROOM'S CHECKLIST (Flowers ordered by bride—bill sent to groom.)								
Bride's bouquet, corsage								
Mother of the bride								
Mother of the groom								
Boutonnieres			Total	$	$	Total	$	$

In Honor of . . .

. . . THE BRIDE

News travels fast—especially news of a wedding. As the wedding day draws near, friends of the bride-to-be begin to think about giving showers in her honor. A shower is a time of celebration when friends can gather for conversing, presenting gifts, and sharing in the bride's excitement.

Usually four to six weeks before the wedding, a close friend of yours, a relative, or a friend of your mother might call to say she would like to give you a bridal shower. (If your mother has a circle of close friends, they will often give showers for each other's daughters. They may invite a few of your friends to attend as well.) The immediate family never gives a shower, but relatives outside the immediate family may. It is not your place to ask for a shower, but hopefully someone will be kind enough to give one for you.

Let your mother know your plans and schedule. That way, if someone calls her, she can give the inquirer an idea of the best time for a shower. Weekends and weekday evenings are usually the most convenient for everyone, unless you are available for a luncheon with nonworking people.

Whoever is giving the shower will want to arrange a suitable date and time with you. She should ask you for a list of the people you would like her to invite. If she doesn't mention a maximum number of guests possible, ask her to specify that. And be sure to keep within those limits. She may ask your preferences regarding the kind of shower that would fill your particular needs, as well as your intended kitchen or bathroom colors. Also, let her know what stores you are registered with for bridal gifts. (For more information on registering, read chapter 10.)

Write out your list promptly, and include addresses and phone numbers with each name. Your hostess doesn't have to know everyone on your list. But it would be helpful to her if you included a word about how each person on the list is related to you. Your mother, the groom's mother, sisters, and soon-to-be sisters-in-law should be invited if they live in the area.

Take care when planning each guest list. A nice size for a group is about a dozen people. If space permits, a larger group is always fun, especially when the guests are related in some particular way (e.g., everyone present works together in the same office). Or several smaller showers may be suggested for convenience' sake.

Unless it is customary for all your attendants to be invited to every shower, you might give them a choice, or request they not bring a gift each time. Inviting other guests to more than one shower puts undue financial pressure on them and is in bad taste.

Only those people on your wedding guest list should be invited to the showers given for you. It is not necessary, though, to include all the wedding guests when planning the showers.

On the other hand, if you are planning a private ceremony and reception for just the families, your friends will understand and may decide to have a shower anyway.

It is customary for some churches to give each bride a shower. It is usually a very special time for all the women of the church, with the bride as the honored guest. Small showers given by individuals will not take the place of this type of shower. While it is difficult to decline the offer, you may turn it down if you are strongly opposed to the idea.

A joint shower for you and your groom, with your friends and his friends attending together, will require making up a guest list together. This type of shower should probably center around items for the house and special interest needs rather than personal gifts—for example, articles for the kitchen, garden, tool chest, or medicine cabinet.

Relatives often have showers where the ladies enjoy the gift giving while the men find an activity by which to entertain the groom. However, the men may enjoy sitting in on the party, too, especially if there are some gifts for the groom. It could be a nice family time enjoyed by all.

If you live out of town, and it is not possible for you to arrive home until a few days before the wedding, it is still possible to attend a shower. This way your friends at home will still be able to share your excitement. However, you will need many helpers to keep you organized at this late date.

If the wedding is to take place a long way from home, some friends will not be able to attend. However, they may want to have a "shower by mail" for you. You and your groom will have a great time opening the gifts and then phoning back immediately to share your excitement and gratitude.

The Shower

It is best to arrive promptly at the time your hostess arranges for you. There should be a special place designated for you to sit. If your mother attends, she should sit on one side of you, and your maid of honor or a close friend on the other side. (See that the groom's mother is seated nearby as well.) They will assist you and keep a record of the gifts as they are opened. Use numbered stickers on each gift to correspond to the number in the Gift Record. It is important also to note the description of the gift on the back of the card. The cards should be left with the gift. Thank the giver immediately, and then pass the gift around the group.

If you're looking for something to do with all that ribbon on the floor, consider using it to make a rehearsal "bouquet." As you open your gifts, have someone tape the bows to a paper plate. Some of the ribbons could also be added cascading down. Now you have a "bouquet" to use during your rehearsal!

It is possible you won't know everyone at a particular shower. For instance, if you attend a large church and a shower is given for you, there will be some ladies whom you may not know by name. If there is someone who knows everyone at the shower, see that she sits near you so that she can clue you in as you are opening the gifts.

When all the gifts are opened, take a moment to thank the group for coming, for their gifts, and for making the occasion so special for you. You may be asked to share a little of how you met your groom, what your courtship was like, and what plans you have for the immediate future. Everyone loves a bride and is interested in these little details.

Have your groom come at the end of the shower so you may introduce him to anyone who hasn't met him. (And he probably won't mind eating that last piece of dessert, either!)

Thank each person again as they leave, and tell them you'll be looking forward to seeing them at the wedding. Wait until everyone has left before packing up the gifts to take them home. Your hostess deserves a big thank you and a call the next day to let her know how nice everything was.

Giving a Shower
Let me take just a moment to talk to those who want to give a shower for a bride. The first thing to do is to call the bride's mother and tell her of your plans.

It is nice to have one shower with the bride's friends, and another with the mother's friends; or, it would be fine to combine these two groups. Relatives often have a separate shower. And sometimes several people will go together to plan a shower, sharing the responsibilities and expenses.

A shower doesn't have to be a formal affair. You could have your guests gather for a potluck supper, coffee and dessert, a barbeque, luncheon, brunch, breakfast, a tea, or even an open house. It could also center around swimming or skiing. Another idea would be to assign each guest an hour of the day and ask her to bring an appropriate gift during her specified hour. The most common type of shower, though, is the evening gathering. However, the time and place are not the important things. The main purpose is to "shower" the bride with gifts.

Make sure to read the preceding section, "The Shower." This will give you a good idea of the information you need to obtain from the bride—date, time, guest list, type of shower she would prefer, color schemes, where she is registered, etc., so you can pass this information on to your guests. If she hasn't registered anywhere, you may suggest she do so. (See chapter 10 for more about registering.) If this is to be a personal shower, ask for her sizes and clothing style preferences.

Plan the shower sometime within six weeks before the wedding. Evening and weekends are usually the best times for guests to attend. Some brides may not appreciate a surprise shower. Since she is in the spotlight, she may want to have some warning in order to look her best. If it *is* to be a surprise, however, the groom should bring the bride after everyone has arrived. He could then be invited to stay for the party.

If there will be a small group attending the shower, you may phone each guest. Otherwise, you should send an invitation containing the extra information you've gleaned (such as size, color scheme, etc.).

Giving a large shower can be quite a project for one person. You may want someone to help you with the shopping, writing, sealing, stamping, and mailing of the invitations. If you don't send the bride an invitation, be sure to give her one later for her wedding book. You may also want to order corsages for the bride and the mothers.

The invitations should be sent out two weeks before the shower, if possible. "Regrets only" and a phone number is the best way to get people to respond.

Ask the guests to come early so the gifts may be arranged ahead of time. Have another table set up somewhere so the gifts may be displayed after the bride has opened them. Decorate the chair for the bride with streamers or a bow. A trash container should be kept ready for the paper and packing materials. Also, have a paper plate or two available on which to fasten rehearsal "bouquets."

There are many possible ways to entertain the guests after the gifts have been opened. First of all, let the bride say a few words of thanks and talk about how she and her groom met. A short talk or devotional given by a close friend or admired older woman is appreciated, followed by prayer for the bride. Last, but not least, there are the refreshments.

Refreshments. Most groups will sit and chat while watching the bride open the gifts. Serving punch during this time is appreciated. If the group is particularly large and there are many gifts to be opened, the bride may enjoy a moment to relax with a cup of punch herself. A simple plate of crackers could be passed around with napkins.

The refreshments may be anything from a simple dessert and beverage to a buffet supper, depending on the time and style of entertaining you prefer. Appropriate decorations and napkins may center around a theme or a color. It is usually not best to use the exact color of the wedding. The bride and her mother may feel awkward if your decorations are more elaborate than their intended reception plans.

Candies and nuts are a customary addition to refreshments. You may also consider some of the newer mixes such as yogurt-covered raisins and nuts, or seeds and raisins. Add a bag of M & Ms or other small candies, and you have a delicious treat.

While planning the menu, think of different flavors, textures, shapes, and colors. Remember to prepare enough for unexpected guests. Will the size and pattern of your plates be appropriate for a party? If not, you may want to borrow some from friends or purchase paper products. If your coffee pot is not large enough, borrow one or serve only punch.

Plan to have refreshments that are not too difficult to make and serve and will not keep you away from the guests too long. Prepare them ahead of time, so you will not continually have to watch your creation in the oven or worry about it burning. You are the hostess, and you want to make as few trips to the kitchen as possible. It is better to let a little etiquette fall by the wayside in favor of good fellowship among your guests.

Set out tablecloths, napkins, and accessories the day before. Arrange for more chairs earlier in the week. Hang your menu in the kitchen. If it is involved, make a time schedule as well. Plan what you will wear and how you will do your hair. By knowing all these details beforehand, you will be able to enjoy your guests and the bride's happiness.

ABC shower ideas. If you're stumped, here are some ideas for shower themes and gifts:

Appliances—small electrical

Bathroom accessories; Books and magazine subscriptions

China

Dust chasers—cloths, spray, mop, vacuum, etc.

Epicurian—canned delicacies

Family—gifts for when the immediate family gathers; your favorite household gadget; a "fix-it" gift.

Garden needs—tools, seeds, hose; Gift certificates

Herbs and spices—have a checklist for guests when they RSVP

Intangible—gifts of song, readings, slide show

Joint—coed for both the bride and groom

Kitchenware—cookware and miscellaneous supplies

Linens—table, bedroom, bathroom

Miscellaneous; Makeup; Mother/daughter

Nature—plants, natural food products

Originals—made by your hands

Personal—lingerie; Pantry; Pottery

Quaint—for a person with Early American taste

Recipe—favorite recipe and the ingredients as a gift

Season tickets (group gift); Sewing accessories; Serving accessories (trays, etc.); Socks and stockings

Travel helps; Tool chest and tools

Useful—anything that is practical

Variety—miscellaneous

Woodenware; Wool

Xtras—impractical, but fun or beautiful things

Yarns—for someone who would appreciate help with projects (The bride should list her preferences.)

ZZZ—bed linens

. . . The Groom

To commemorate his "farewell to bachelorhood," friends of the groom may treat him to dinner or a sports event. This custom varies from place to place, and should be done several days before the wedding.

A relative or friend may choose to plan a golf outing and lunch on the day of the wedding. Some groups like to stay up late the night before. While this may be fun, everyone involved should remember the responsibilities they will be expected to perform the next day.

. . . The Bridesmaids

A nice custom is to have a luncheon on the day of the rehearsal, after everyone has arrived for the wedding. It will be a special time for you and your bridesmaids to be together. Any from out of town may be introduced to the others at this time, too. You can give your attendants their thank-you gifts during this luncheon, or you can give them at the rehearsal dinner.

You could have an informal luncheon at home with a menu of quiche or crepes. Otherwise, Chinese or Mexican restaurants are always fun places to go. Wherever you have this luncheon, make sure the place is brightly lit. This will lift everyone's spirits, and add to the excitement.

A menu that is light on the condiments will be best for any nervous stomachs. Hold back on the coffee—drink a glass of milk instead.

An old tradition is to have pink cake served for dessert with a ring or a thimble baked into it. As custom goes, whoever gets the piece with the item in it will be the next bride-to-be.

There are many last-minute items that need to be tended to during these last few days. Therefore, you should arrange for this time with your bridesmaids to be at an early hour. That way there will still be time to pick up a gown or go for that last fitting. If there is time, you may invite everyone back to your place to see the gifts that have been received.

... THE WEDDING PARTY

A dinner the night before the wedding is usually held to honor you, your groom, and the members of your wedding party. Usually referred to as the rehearsal dinner, this event is really the beginning of the wedding celebration, because this is the first time that everyone involved has a chance to sit together. People from out of town will feel part of the festivities as they are introduced at this time.

This event may take the form of a formal dinner, informal supper, or light refreshments, but should follow the style of the wedding. Any gifts you wish to give your attendants and others could be given at this time.

The groom's parents are responsible for this dinner, which is held before or after the rehearsal. (Having it after the rehearsal allows for a more relaxing time together.) The people attending would be the members of the bridal party, their spouses, both sets of parents and other immediate family members, any relatives from out of town, grandparents, the minister and his spouse, and the parents of any children attendants. (You do not *have* to invite the musicians and their spouses.) Other than the young attendants, children are usually not included.

If the groom's parents are from out of town, you may have to do part of the planning. They may want you to suggest a place to hold the affair. Suggest several places, and send them menus from each. This way they may see the range of prices and make their decision accordingly. Many restaurants and clubs are prepared for this type of dinner. On the other hand, a nice choice might be a dinner in the church parlor.

Another alternative location for the rehearsal dinner may be the home of either set of parents. But keep in mind that an elaborate party is a great deal of work, and whoever hosts the dinner may be tired and irritable the next day.

Wherever the dinner is held, it is best to hold it at a place that is convenient and not too far away.

Begin by making two guest lists—one of those people you "must invite" and the other of "optional" guests. You may need to limit the number because of space or expense. Include the addresses, phone numbers, and how each person fits into the wedding plans. The groom's parents will want to send or phone the invitations several weeks in advance.

Next, reserve the location and a caterer, if needed. Select the menu, write the place cards, and plan a seating arrangement. A centerpiece and candles for the main table add a festive touch. If the place is difficult to find, have a map drawn up to be given out at the rehearsal. All of this should be taken care of by the groom's mother if she lives in the area.

The best man can be the moderator. After one of the fathers or the minister gives thanks for the food, it is proper for the fathers to give a greeting, a salute to the coming marriage. This is an ideal time for other family members to bestow their good wishes, also. Remember though, lengthy orations are out of place.

After dinner, a *short* slide show of the bride's and groom's childhood days would be amusing. This should be carefully planned so that it does not become too drawn out and boring.

Before everyone leaves for the night, any final reminders for the next day should be given. You may want to let everyone know about transportation to the reception, formation of the receiving line, etc. Write these reminders out and have your moderator announce them.

Planning the Rehearsal Dinner

Below is a checklist for anyone who is hosting a rehearsal dinner:

1. Consult with the bride and groom to determine the date and time.
2. Ask the bride for a guest list. Let her know of any space and/or budget restrictions. Ask her to include addresses, phone numbers, and the role each person plays in the wedding.
3. If you are from out of town, ask the bride for suggestions on where to hold the dinner and for copies of the menus from each place.
4. Reserve the room, select a menu, plan a seating arrangement, write place cards, and purchase a centerpiece and candles for the main table.
5. The invitations should be sent two weeks in advance. If you telephone the guests, a postcard serves as a nice reminder.
6. Ask the bride if she would like any type of program to be presented. Otherwise, your best wishes and words of encouragement could be given, followed by a word from the fathers or mothers.
7. Arrange for a moderator, and someone to ask the blessing.
8. The day of the dinner, go to the site

and check on the details (decorations, tables, seating, parking facilities, and place cards).

REHEARSAL DINNER
Diagram of seating

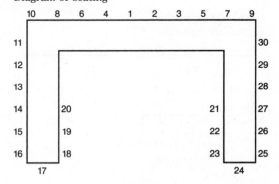

1. Bride
2. Groom
3. Maid of Honor
4. Best man
5. Usher/groomsman
6. Bridesmaid
7. Bridesmaid
8. Usher/groomsman
9. Usher/groomsman
10. Bridesmaid
11. Usher/groomsman
12. Bride's aunt
13. Junior usher/groomsman
14. Minister's wife
15. Groom's grandfather
16. Bride's grandmother
17. Groom's father (host)
18. Bride's mother
19. Godfather
20. Usher's wife
21. Bridesmaid's husband
22. Godmother
23. Minister
24. Groom's mother (hostess)

25. Bride's father
26. Groom's grandmother
27. Bride's uncle
28. Groom's cousin
29. Junior usher
30. Bridesmaid

REHEARSAL DINNER
or Informal Reception

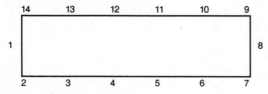

1. Groom's father (host)
2. Bride's mother
3. Usher
4. Best man's wife
5. Bride's brother
6. Bridesmaid
7. Bride's grandfather
8. Groom's mother (hostess)
9. Bride's father
10. Maid of honor
11. Groom
12. Bride
13. Best man
14. Bride's grandmother

. . . YOUR HELPERS
You might consider having everyone who is helping with the wedding and reception over to your home for a yard-long submarine sandwich. Any final instructions could be given then. Or, you may be so involved before the wedding that you don't get a chance to say thank you to those people who will help with your wedding, who had a shower for you, or who entertained for you. One way to show your appreciation in this case would be to have them all over after you return from your honeymoon.

It could be a simple affair, with only vegetables, chips and dip, and root beer floats. You could share with them any honeymoon and wedding pictures you have. Even if your home isn't settled or decorated yet, your warm hospitality is all that matters. They have given of their time to help make your wedding a success, and your appreciation should be evident.

. . . THE PARENTS
You and your groom should arrange to spend some time alone with each set of parents before the wedding day. This would be one way of expressing your appreciation and love. It can be dinner together, a walk, or going for an ice cream cone. Whatever you do, the time will be memorable because it is time you are setting aside to be with them in the midst of the hectic plans.

. . . OUT-OF-TOWN GUESTS
A luncheon or brunch on the day of the wedding could be arranged for out-of-town guests. Your presence would not be required. A neighbor or good friend may offer to entertain them while you are involved with the last-minute details of your wedding. One way to do this is to take them on a tour of the area in a van or station wagon.

Gifts & Thank Yous

REGISTERING FOR GIFTS

It has become a customary practice in most parts of the country to register your gift preferences at a local department store or gift shop. It is not only a convenience for the wedding and shower guests, but it also relieves the problem of duplicate gifts.

A bridal gift registry is a free service. A gift consultant is usually available to give her expert advice in answer to your questions about the merchandise, but you may need to make an appointment with her. She will be available to help you select suitable sizes, patterns, and coordinating color combinations, if you desire. She will also see that your selections are listed and sent to branch stores, if they exist.

You may find it embarrassing to make a list of the gifts people could give you. By doing this, however, you are giving those who care about you the chance to give you what you really want and need. Just be sure that you make your selections with a wide range of prices available. Specialty shops for kitchenware and bathroom accessories will usually have this wide price range, as well as a large selection of colors and styles. Registering at more than one store is preferable for the various tastes of your guests. You should register in your fiancé's hometown as well as your own, or give his mother a list of your needs.

If you are completely opposed to the idea of the bridal gift registry, give your mother and close friends an idea of the things you already have so they can answer the questions of friends and relatives who want to know your needs.

If you want to be registered somewhere, take time to look around first. With your groom, try to decide on the style of living you both like or might like in the future. Do some research on different living styles by looking at store displays and model homes. Go to the library to browse through the many home furnishing magazines. Then together pick out patterns, colors, bed size, etc.

Traditional household furnishings give a home a formal look. This particular style never seems to go out of date. This is where the finest quality of material and workmanship is used. You may want to stay with that feeling in your living room, dining room, and bedroom areas. Just remember, polishing silver and furniture is also a part of this life-style.

For a more comfortable, relaxed style of living, a country or Early American decor is best.

An eclectic style or a combination of old and new can give you many different decorating opportunities and relieves any budget pressures as you begin gathering household items. A basic color could be used throughout the house, with contrasting accents in different rooms. It will give your home a smooth, connected feeling, even in the smallest living quarters. Warm colors instantly give a feeling of optimism and happiness, and are wonderful for gloomy days.

Your selection of major items such as fine china, sterling silver, or silverplate will take some contemplation and perhaps more than one trip to the store. It is possible that your groom's tastes are entirely different from yours. But if you search long enough you are likely to find something you can both agree on. Or, possibly your groom may let you choose whatever you like. This is an area where you will need to use good, unhurried judgment. If you choose something you're sure you really like, you will always enjoy it.

Another thought on choosing china and silver is to try and think long range. Is this pattern time tested? Has it been around a long time and will it likely be available in five or ten years when you need a few replacement pieces? If it's "faddish," it may be discontinued in a short time, and become unavailable for replacements.

It is perfectly acceptable to register for high quality and high priced items if you expect to do formal entertaining. (It is difficult to know that now, especially if you are struggling financially.) If you do not plan to entertain formally, there are beautiful semiformal porcelains, or the more casual stonewares. The stainless steel flatware has a mellow, durable beauty. It is wise also to look into open stock patterns.

If you and your groom have decided to do missionary work in another country, you are probably wondering what would be practical for you to register for. Carol Jean headed for the mission field as a young bride. She and her husband were called upon to do a great amount of entertaining. Therefore, she was glad she had received gifts of china, silverware, and linens to handle these entertaining opportunities. Even her silver candleholders received a lot of use.

On the mission field, you might find that your home will become a lodging place for overnight guests. This task usually falls to the married couples more than to the single people, so it would be best to be prepared. You will need extra quantities of dishes, silverware, and glasses. There are usually no good paper products available, so washable placemats, tablecloths, and napkins are always practical items to have around. An especially exquisite or expensive wedding gift may have to be stored away for a future furlough time or some later year.

RECEIVING GIFTS

Receiving shower and wedding gifts, shopping and buying, you can accumulate more than you ever dreamed or cared to own! Think of the people behind each gift, the ones who want to share this very important moment with you. These are their expressions of love for your enjoyment in the years ahead.

Local customs often dictate whether gifts are sent to the bride's home or brought to the church or reception. Sending gifts to the home is the traditional and proper way. However, the practicality of bringing them to the church cannot be denied. Many stores either do not deliver or charge a delivery fee. Therefore, many guests might prefer to hand-deliver them personally.

If you don't want gifts sent to your home, give a different return address on your invitation (possibly your parents' home). You could also ask the store where you have registered if they would hold any gifts for a certain length of time before delivering them.

Gifts usually begin arriving as soon as the invitations are sent out. It's fun tearing open the card to see who the gift is from, opening the white wrappings and silver ribbons, and enjoying the surprise someone has planned for you. Sharing this experience with your groom will make it all the more exciting.

If there is no card, look for a clue such as the postmark or the store where it was purchased. If you contact the store right away, they may have a record of the person who purchased it.

Continue listing the gifts in your Gift Record that you started at your showers, using numbered stickers on each gift. Record the description of the gift, the store from which it came, and the date with the corresponding number of the sticker. Write the description on the back of each card as well, and keep the cards in a separate box or tape them to the gifts. Warranty and rebate cards or instructions should be kept in a safe place.

It is always best to open the gifts yourself, but this may not always be possible. If you are at school or out of town until the wedding, you may give your mother or a friend permission to open your gifts, display, and record them if they are sent to their home. A printed acknowledgment card may then be sent in your maiden name if you wish.

Here is an example:

Mr. and Mrs. (your parents' name)
or
Miss (your name)
wishes to acknowledge
the receipt of your kind gift
and will send a personal note
at a later date.

Damaged Gifts

A gift that arrives damaged should be handled in one of the following ways:

- Notify the store that it came from and ask about their policies for damaged merchandise.
- If the gift is insured, notify the donor of its condition.
- If it is not insured and there is nothing to identify where it was purchased, you should assume that the donor sent the gift in perfect condition and that it was damaged en route to you. Unless the giver asks about it, you will have to assume the loss yourself.

Exchanging Gifts

Exchanging a gift can be a touchy issue. If the gift is a duplicate or if you can exchange it for something more useful to you, then do so. However, exchanging for a cash refund is in very poor taste. A gift from a close friend or relative should never be exchanged without permission.

DISPLAYING GIFTS

If displaying your gifts in your home is the custom where you live, you will need to set aside a specific place. It would be best to have all the gifts contained in one area, if possible, and arranged tastefully in a color-coordinated theme. Tables with cloths to the floor make lovely displays to show off your gifts. The boxes, covers, and packing materials may be stored underneath. You may choose whether or not to display the cards along with the gifts. Only one of any particular item need be displayed.

It isn't necessary to display the shower gifts, but if you wish to, they should be together in a separate place.

If you don't display the gifts, write a brief description of each one on the outside of the box. Keep your gifts in the boxes they came in. This will help you when you are storing things away or moving them.

AT THE RECEPTION

At large weddings where time and energy are important factors, a popular custom is to have several friends unwrap the gifts at the reception and display them while the bride and groom are in the receiving line. Someone else can be appointed to collect monetary gifts in a satin sack. This whole procedure is acceptable when there are hundreds of guests or when there is limited space (as in the home of the bride), but it should be used as a last resort. The giving and receiving of a gift has great significance. If at all possible, you and your groom should personally acknowledge each guest's thoughtfulness by opening the gift yourselves.

You should be aware of this responsibility if you decide on a large, formal wedding. Time should be allowed for the opening of the gifts. It may be an extra burden to have to fit this in when you are wanting to leave for your honeymoon,

but it really should be done before you go. As you open each gift, remember the last one is as important as the first.

If for some reason you don't have time to open all of the gifts and you are planning to take an extended wedding trip, it would be good to have an engraved or printed acknowledgment card sent to those donors whose gifts you have not opened. A phone call from your mother would be another nice way to acknowledge them.

There are at least two different ways to handle the opening of gifts:

1. Wait until the reception is over. Your closest friends and relatives can watch you open your gifts and help pack them away to be taken to an appointed place.

2. Take all of the gifts home and have a gift-opening time before you leave. Your attendants will no doubt gather at your home to wait for you to change and to see you off.

You could set a specific time to stop opening if you really must leave. Everyone will understand when you say, "Thank you so very much, but we really must go." Another party can be arranged for after the honeymoon so that the rest of the gifts can be opened.

CALLING IT OFF

When a wedding is called off or an engagement broken, wedding gifts are returned to the sender. The gift should be sent directly to the sender rather than the store from which it was purchased. A note of thanks and a quick word saying you decided to call it off are all that is needed. You should send back the gifts from *your* friends, and he sends back those gifts from *his* friends. If he is out of town and all the gifts have been sent to you, you will have to return them.

Prewedding shower gifts to the bride may be kept. However, a verbal explanation is always nice. Gifts should be kept also if a wedding is postponed because of extenuating circumstances, unless it is postponed indefinitely.

GIFTS FOR THOSE INVOLVED IN YOUR WEDDING

A gift from you and your groom for services rendered is a special way to say an extra thank you to those who help with the wedding. Boutonnieres and corsages may be sent to the men and women taking part, along with an invitation to the rehearsal dinner. (The invitation is a nice gesture, but not necessary.)

If you have any high-ranking persons, such as a mayor or governor, officiating at the wedding as a personal favor, any gift will be appreciated. However, a note of thanks would be sufficient.

A gift to a bridesmaid is a token of remembrance of your wedding. A piece of

BRIDE'S GIFT CHECKLIST

NAME	GIFT	EST. COST	ACTUAL COST
Maid of Honor			
Bridesmaids			
Jr. Bridesmaids			
Flower Girl			
Groom			
Parents			
Other			
Total		$ ___	$ ___

jewelry engraved with the date of the wedding on the back is considered to be a cherished memento. Even a young flower girl will treasure a shiny necklace.

However, a practical gift may be more to your liking and is certain to be appreciated, also. If you wish, you can purchase the bridesmaids' dresses for them. If they are carrying silk flower bouquets, you may present them with these lovely flowers as a gift to be used as a centerpiece for many years to come. A necklace or bracelet to be worn for the wedding is often given. Anything that is monogrammed or handmade is also nice.

The ushers and best man will be appreciative of having their wedding attire paid for as a gift. However, if that is impossible, a personal accessory would be the best choice (a belt buckle, pewter mug, etc.). A less sentimental gift would be tickets to a sports event. Remember the ring bearer—a small gift for a small boy.

You may give both sets of parents a small gift to say, "Thank you; we love you." Find something that each parent would enjoy, such as a flowering house plant or an engraved door knocker for the front door. Or you may order flowers to be sent to them after the wedding.

A sentimental custom of a bride and groom presenting a gift to each other on the night before the wedding continues on. The gift should be of long-lasting significance as a reminder of the day. An example would be a piece of jewelry engraved with a few special words. Of course a more practical gift is totally acceptable, but may not have the same permanence as jewelry. These gifts are not essential, and with all the other wedding expenses they may not be realistic.

One young man had his vows written in beautiful calligraphy and framed for his bride. He wrapped it the night before, but decided to have it delivered to her dressing room just before the wedding. It was a tender moment when she opened it.

YOUR WRITTEN THANKS

Supplies

Notepaper. The thank-you notes should be folded notes, either plain or of a conservative color. (The shower gift thank-you notes can be more decorative.) The notes should be blank inside, giving you plenty of room to write your personal words. Notes with verses already printed on them should not be used. Informal notes with only your first names can be printed up. These can then be used before and after the wedding. Or you may contact certain photographers who can put your wedding picture on the front of a thank-you note. However, you will find this to be much more expensive than ordinary thank-you notes. Your notes may be late in getting out to your friends, as well, because you will have to wait until after your pictures have been developed.

If having your picture on the thank-you note is important to you, then you might consider having an informal pose taken long before the wedding. This way, the person making up the notes for you will have plenty of time.

Stamps. The post office often has a floral or love theme stamp which is nice for weddings.

Pen. Use black or blue ink.

Gift Record. Be sure to keep a list of donors' names and description of gifts.

Card file. Record gift descriptions and date of acknowledgment on individual

3″ x 5″ donor cards. (See chapter 16, "Checklists and Worksheets.")

Have all your supplies set aside in a special place so you may sit down each day to catch up on your notes.

When to Write

You will be writing thank-you notes from the time your engagement is announced until several weeks after the wedding. Write as promptly as possible. It's best if each gift is acknowledged within two weeks from the time you receive it. Three months would be the outside limit. When you see that person on the street or in the receiving line, continue to say thank-you. No time is wrong for expressing gratitude.

If a gift or card is accidentally misplaced and turns up later, a note should be written to the donor immediately. Apologies should be made, along with a brief explanation and your thanks for the gift.

Who Writes

A personal thank-you note must be written for each gift received, whether or not you have given your verbal thanks. You may sign it either with your first name (for friends and relatives) or with your full name (for those you do not know). Your groom should be mentioned in each note, also.

If you are employed and are falling behind on the notes, your groom could write the notes to people only he knows, and for the gifts addressed to you both. He, then, would be the one to sign them, while mentioning you in the notes.

In case you are going on an extended vacation, or you are away at school, an acknowledgment card should be sent when the gift arrives. A personal thank-you note is still required at a later time, though.

To Whom

Traditionally, if the gift is from a couple, you should address the note to the wife and mention her husband in the note. Sending a thank-you note to a whole family can be somewhat tricky. Instead of saying, "Dear Aunt Esther, Uncle Bart, Gayle, Gary, and Gregg," say, "Dear Aunt Esther, Jeff and I want to thank you, Uncle Bart, and your whole family for the. . . ."

If you receive a gift "from the group," address the thank-you note to the head of the department or organization. Ask them to thank everyone, and then try to thank each person verbally as you see him or her.

If a group of friends sends one gift but individually list their names on the card, send each one a thank-you note.

Engagement gifts are not as common, but if someone sends you one, a personal note should be written. Thank all those who send you written congratulations *verbally,* in person or by phone.

If you do not give a gift of some kind to each person taking part in your wedding, at least send each a thank-you note. That list should include shower and party hostesses.

If close friends have given you more than one gift, you need to send only one note saying, "Thank you for everything you've done for us."

Sending a note of thanks to both sets of parents is not necessary, but the unexpected is always nice.

How

Each note should be written by hand in the order that the gifts were received.

Your Gift Record (in chapter 16) will be of great help here. The note doesn't have to be long, but your enthusiasm at receiving the gift should be evident.

The elements of a thank-you note are:

- Thanks from you and your husband.
- Mention what the gift was. (If you don't know what it is, refer to the material that it is made of or its shape.) If the gift was money, don't mention the specific amount; just say, "Thank you for your kind gift of money."
- Say something else about the gift, e.g., your reaction when you first received it, the beauty of it, what you're going to do with it, etc.
- Thank the donor again and sign off.

Why

In 1 Timothy 4:4 it says, "Everything created by God is good, and nothing is to be rejected if it is received with thanksgiving" (RSV). There are many incidences in Scripture that point out the importance of being thankful for all things.

Jesus Christ gave thanks to the Father in every area of life. Let us follow His example.

To the Wedding Guest

Any invitation or announcement you receive should be acknowledged with at least a card. If you will be giving a gift, either mail it to the return address on the invitation or take it with you to the wedding. If a whole family has been invited to the wedding, only one gift is necessary.

If you are sending the gift before the wedding, the card should be addressed to the bride in her maiden name. The card should be addressed to the new husband and wife if you are taking the gift to the wedding or sending it afterward. If you are bringing a check as a gift, entrust it to the best man for safekeeping.

Gifts from Parents

Parents usually give gifts of personal or household items. Sometimes either family may present the bride with a piece of heirloom jewelry. The wedding itself, however, is considered to be the bride's parents' gift (if they paid for it). Often the bride's family will also pay for her trousseau and a gift of silver or china.

Traditionally, the silver is given by the bride's parents. Today, with the high cost of silver, she may receive only a start from her parents, and other guests may add to it.

The groom's parents should consider giving a substantial gift of silver, china, or furnishings, if possible.

Invitations

The day will finally arrive when you will mail out your wedding invitations—but not until many hours have been invested in making up the guest list, selecting the invitations, and addressing them.

Whatever the style, wording, or design, all invitations should convey basic information. It is usually stated in the third person, in this way:

- Name or names of persons giving the wedding
- The full names of the bride and groom
- The date and time
- The location of the ceremony
- R.S.V.P. (or R.s.v.p.)
- Place and time of reception (optional)

If the purely traditional, formal style is desired, choose your stationer from the many who carry a complete line of wedding stationery (i.e., gift shops, stationery stores, card stores, bridal shops, print shops). Look at the samples they have available. Select one, choose the color and typeface, and the number you desire. Then talk with the store owner. He may be able to advise you on the quality of the paper stock and formal wording. Prices will vary with quality.

An invitation with more contemporary wording may also be made up in the for-

mal style. It will relay a message from the bride and groom not found in some traditional invitations.

An informal invitation style sets the tone for a more informal wedding. If you are planning a small wedding, the invitations may be written by hand or telephoned by your mother or close friend. If the wedding is small and the reception large, send a reception invitation with the same formal wording, with "reception" replacing the word "wedding."

Here is an example of a handwritten invitation:

Dear Kerry and Linda:
Mark and I are to be married at Faith Church on May twentieth at two-thirty. We hope you both will come to the church and afterward to the reception in the lower auditorium.

Our sincere love,
Sarah and Mark

In the case that you choose to invite only a few people to the reception, handwrite the word "reception" (followed by the location and time) on the bottom of the invitations going to those particular people.

If the wedding and the reception are

held in the same place, a separate invitation is not needed.

ORDERING

As soon as you announce your engagement, both families should start making out their guest lists. The combined lists will be your final number. Order one invitation for each married couple, and one for each single adult over thirteen years of age. As you count, consider any variations in the way you divide your invitations (e.g., wedding only, reception only, etc.). Keep them in separate sections. Order a few extra invitations for keepsakes and any last-minute needs.

At the risk of stating the obvious, double-check to see that both the date and time are confirmed with the minister. Finalize the wedding site and the reception location *before* ordering your invitations.

The stationer will have many styles to offer you. The classic invitation is on a traditional white or ivory-colored stock, in a heavy quality bond, vellum, or parchment. This can be engraved, printed, or thermographed with the typeface you desire, in lettering or script. Calligraphy has gained popularity in recent years. An invitation may be done this way and then taken to the printer for copying.

The use of tissue inside the invitation is optional. The original purpose of using the tissue was to prevent the ink from smearing. However, the ink will be dry by the time you receive the invitations, so the tissue is not necessary.

Whether you decide on plain or bordered stock, consider how many letters you have to get into the available space. Invitations in sizes 5½″ x 7½″ or 4½″ x 5¾″ are used most often.

When ordering, ask for a guarantee of replacement. This insures that there will be no extra charge in case of a misprint. You may also ask that the delivery date be guaranteed.

WORDING THE INVITATION

A traditional formal wedding invitation would be worded like this:

(A) *Mr. and Mrs. Christopher Lee Parsons*
(B) *request the honour of your presence*
(C) *at the marriage of their daughter*
(D) *Sarah Joanne*
to
(E) *Mr. Mark Andrew Kingdon*
(F) *Saturday, the twelfth of May*
(G) *nineteen hundred and eighty-four*
(H) *at half after two o'clock*
(I) *in the afternoon*
(J) *Faith Church*
(K) *Concord at Madison*
(L) *Glasston, Michigan*
(M) *Reception at four o'clock*
(N) *Lower auditorium*
(O) *R.s.v.p.*

Notice the only punctuation used is after Mr. and Mrs. and to divide the day and date, city and state.

The following are correct wordings for each of the lines.
(A) *"MR. AND MRS. CHRISTOPHER LEE PARSONS"*
1. Titles:
a. Should be used if a man is called by his title (i.e., Doctor [M.D.], Judge, the Reverend), and should be written out.

The academic degree is usually not used.

b. Mothers never use a title on their daughter's wedding invitation.

c. Mothers use a title (Doctor, etc.) only when the invitation is issued in the name of the bride and groom.

d. A professional name may be given in parentheses below the given name.

e. Use your father's title or the groom's father's title if he is a high-ranking member of the army, navy, coast guard, marine corps, or on active duty in the reserve forces. Example:

Captain Rex Lloyd

United States Army

f. Those with ranks below captain in the army or lieutenant, senior grade, in the navy have rank written below the name. Example:

Matthew Hicks

Ensign, United States Navy

g. For a reserve officer on active duty, the second line would read:

Army of the United States

or

United States Naval Reserve

h. Both first and second lieutenants in the army use "Lieutenant" without numerals.

i. An enlisted man may or may not use his title and branch of service on the line below his name. Example:

Allen Whiteford

Sergeant

Medical Corps, United States

j. High-ranking retired army or navy officers retain their titles in civilian life.

k. A bride in military service usually does not use her title, but she may if she likes.

l. A degree that is to be received (e.g., medical, law) by the time of the wedding may be used on the invitation.

2. The full name must always be written out.

3. Even if the wedding is to take place in a friend's home, the invitations should be issued in the name of the parents or sponsors. The name and address of the residence should be given on the lower left-hand corner.

4. When the parents are divorced:

a. The mother uses her first and married or maiden name. It is not necessary to include both maiden and married name.

b. If the mother and father give the wedding as co-hosts, both names should appear separately (and may include any new spouses' names), with the mother's name appearing first.

c. The mother can give the wedding and the father can give the reception. This should be indicated accordingly on the invitation and reception card.

5. If the bride is an orphan and the

wedding is given by others:
a. The friends' names are given in the place of the parents.
b. If a brother, sister, or other relative is giving the wedding, then his or her name should be used.
6. If the bride and groom send out their own invitations, the invitation can begin with:
a. "The honour of your presence is requested by . . ." or
b. "Miss Sarah Joanne Parsons and Mr. Mark Andrew Kingdon request the honour of your presence. . . ."
c. If your parents are living, however, every consideration should be given to having their names on the invitation, even if they are not giving the wedding.
7. A divorcee or widow of maturity may issue the invitations in her own name, or begin it with: "The honour of your presence is requested at the marriage of Mrs. Mary Appleton. . . ."
8. In the event of a double wedding, the parents' name is given; or in the case of two brides who are friends, both sets of parents' names appear on the invitations. For example:

Mr. and Mrs. Jay Benning

Mr. and Mrs. Thomas Dow

request the honour of your presence

at the marriage of their daughters

Barbara Denise

to Mr. Bartholomew Daly

and

Cheryl Elaine

to Mr. Ryan Daniels

Saturday, the seventh of January

nineteen hundred and eighty-four

at two' o'clock

Community Bible Church

Larkin, Montana

9. If the parents of the groom give the wedding:
a. Their name should appear on the first line. This is acceptable in the event that the bride's parents are in another country, are deceased, or if they disapprove of the marriage.
b. The groom's parents may offer their assistance whatever the situation may be, but the bride's parents' name should appear on the first line of the invitation.
10. If both sets of parents give the wedding, then both names should appear on the invitation.

(B) *"REQUEST THE HONOUR OF YOUR PRESENCE"*

These spellings of "honour" and "favour" are used for a formal, religious setting. If the wedding is taking place somewhere other than a church, the wording would be "request the pleasure of your company."

(C) *"AT THE MARRIAGE OF THEIR DAUGHTER"*

1. If the mother is widowed or has remarried, it may read "her daughter." Her name and new spouse's name would appear on the first line. On the other hand, if the mother is widowed and not remarried, it may still read "their daughter."

2. If the bride and groom are giving the wedding, this may read, "at their marriage."

3. "At the marriage of their niece" is used when an aunt and uncle are giving the wedding.

(D) *"SARAH JOANNE"*

1. "Miss Sarah Joanne Parsons" would be used when there are no relatives and friends are giving the wedding.

2. When a young widow is remarrying, her former married name is used: "Sarah Parsons Kelly." Parents may send the formal invitations.

3. Double wedding: Both of the brides' names appear, joined by an "and." (See example on p. 80.)

(E) *"MR. MARK ANDREW KINGDON"*

Titles may be used for the groom. Always use the full name.

(F) *"SATURDAY, THE TWELFTH OF MAY"*

An invitation should never read "May 12th."

(G) *"NINETEEN HUNDRED AND EIGHTY-FOUR"*

The year should always be written out, following this form.

(H) *"AT HALF AFTER TWO O'CLOCK"*

It should not be "two-thirty" or "half past two."

(I) *"IN THE AFTERNOON"*

Or "in the morning" or "in the evening," if appropriate.

(J) *"FAITH CHURCH"*

Use the church's name as it appears in the Sunday morning bulletin.

(K) *"CONCORD AT MADISON"*

The street number is not written out. Any surrounding streets may also be named.

(L) *"GLASSTON, MICHIGAN"*

No zip code is needed. Notice that the state is completely written out.

(M) *"RECEPTION AT FOUR O'CLOCK"*

1. If the reception is to follow immediately after the ceremony, then the time of the reception is not given. The time should be given in the case where there will be a lapse between the ceremony and reception to allow for pictures to be taken.

2. A morning reception would be called a "breakfast" or "brunch" if a meal is served.

(N) *"LOWER AUDITORIUM"*

The location of the reception is given here. However, if the reception is a sit-down affair, a separate reception card should be enclosed.

(O) *"R.s.v.p." (or "R.S.V.P.")*

"Reply please" or "The favour of a reply is requested" would also be correct. This may be followed by "Kindly send reply to . . . ," followed by a name and address if it differs from the return address on the envelope.

Use the space below to plan your invitation:

SAMPLE INVITATIONS

God
who is love Himself
has brought
Odette Binder
and
Michael Trabor
together in His love
Mr. and Mrs. Richard Thomas
would be pleased to have you attend
the ceremony making them
one
in marriage
September 7, at two o'clock
in the afternoon
First Baptist Church
Merrillville, Minnesota

Believing marriage to be ordained
by God
Ruth Marie
and
Robert Edson
together with our parents
Mr. and Mrs. Daniel Melton
and
Mr. and Mrs. Caleb Miles
invite you to worship with us
and witness our vows
as we are united in Christ
Saturday, September twenty-first
at four o'clock in the afternoon

Lakewood Bible Church
722 South Wrightwood Drive
Whitesburg, Massachusetts
If you are unable to attend
we ask your presence in thought
and prayer
Reception following

ADDRESSING THE INVITATIONS

The Outer Envelope

Ask that the envelopes be delivered to the store as soon as possible, even if the invitations haven't been printed yet. This way you can get an early start on addressing them.

The addresses should be handwritten by the bride in black ink, or you may wish to use the color of the ink used on the invitation. If the guest list is large, you may have to enlist the help of your mother, maid of honor, or others, or possibly hire a secretary. The addresses should never be typed.

If you have only a few to be addressed, you may want to hire a calligrapher. He would charge by the piece, and could cost from a dollar on up for the two envelopes.

Abbreviations should not be used when writing the names. The person's middle name may be used if you like. If it *is* used, it should be written out in full. Titles are also written out, as are "Avenue," "Street," the city, and state. The zip code is most important—if you don't know a particular zip code, check with the post office or get a zip code directory.

"The Smith Family" is not proper. Instead, the parents' names should be written out. If there is no inner envelope, then the daughters' names would follow with "Misses" preceding their names. Young boys' names would be added as "Messrs." or "Masters" and then their full names.

Remember, both members of a couple should be invited, even if you only know one of them.

The Inner Envelope

The inner envelope is optional, but is usually included with a formal invitation. It should be addressed with the last name of a couple, such as "Mr. and Mrs. Dunton." If there are children invited under the age of fifteen, their first names should be written underneath each other in the order of age.

If you are not pressed for space at the church and your budget can afford it, you may add "and guest" on the invitation of a single person. This may also be added on the outside envelope if there is no inner envelope. Otherwise, you could include a personal note to that effect.

On the inner envelope, very close relatives may be addressed as "Grandma" or "Aunt Dorothy," etc.

RETURN ADDRESSES

The return address may be engraved or printed on the upper left-hand corner of the outside envelope. (The postal authorities prefer this, but it is not a law.) Or a blind embosser may be purchased at the stationer's store for printing the return address on the outside flap. This can be used for many years, and the address may be changed as needed.

If an invitation is returned because the address was wrong, make the change, if possible, and send it out again (if it is not too late). It would be best to phone the

people also, and express your desire for them to come.

ENCLOSURES

Reception Card

This is a small card containing the information about the reception, such as time and location. It is usually used if a luncheon or dinner is to be held. It is enclosed with the invitation.

RECEPTION CARD

> *Luncheon served*
> *at one thirty o'clock*
> *Crossley Country Club*

Response Card and Envelope

This card is enclosed for the guest's convenience in accepting or declining your invitation to the reception. A stamped envelope which has the return address already on it should be included.

Pew Card

Pew cards are used only for very large weddings. They are small cards with pew numbers printed on them; or, they may say, "Within the ribbon."

A pew card is sent to a guest after you have received his acceptance. (The bride's and groom's first names must be on it.) The guest is then expected to present this card to the usher at the wedding. This entitles the guest to a reserved seat in a certain pew.

Pew cards are usually unnecessary because ushers can simply reserve certain pews for relatives and close friends of the bride and groom.

PEW CARD

```
+-------------------------------------------+
|          Please present this card         |
|                Faith Church               |
|         Saturday, the twentieth of May    |
|                                           |
|      Pew #6    Greg and Jennifer          |
+-------------------------------------------+
```

Admission Card
These are used in the case of a celebrity being married, where the ceremony is open to the public. Otherwise, they are used if the wedding is held in a public place where there are sightseers.

At Home Card
These cards are used to let the guests know when the bride and groom will be moving into their new residence. Therefore, they should include the date and address. For example:

At Home

after July fifth

23 Essex Court

Bellingham, California 99982

STUFFING THE ENVELOPES
The invitation should be inserted with the folded edge first and the front of the invitation facing the flap. Any enclosures are inserted facing the flap, in front of the invitation. In the large double-sheet folded invitations, the enclosures are inserted inside the fold.

The inner envelope should not have any form of adhesion on the flap. After the enclosures and invitation have been placed in the inner envelope, this envelope is placed in the outer envelope. The names should be facing the flap. The out-

er envelope can then be sealed and mailed.

Remember to *check each envelope* before sealing to make sure it contains the invitation.

One couple learned this lesson the hard way, not with their invitations, but with their wedding announcements. On the day before the wedding, the bride went out for a few last errands. She asked the groom to seal and stamp the announcements in preparation for sending them out after the wedding. She had unwisely decided not to put a return address on them. The groom happily sealed and stamped each envelope. After the wedding, the whole stack went out on time.

Some time later, a pile of announcements were found in their original box. Too late, the bride and groom realized that not all the envelopes they had sent out had been stuffed. It was never determined just who received those empty envelopes!

MAILING THE INVITATIONS
All of the invitations should be addressed and mailed first class so that they arrive no later than two weeks before the wedding. Four to six weeks is not too soon for an invitation to an ultraformal wedding to be mailed out. Notes for an informal wedding may be sent ten days before.

Weigh one invitation with all the enclosures, then purchase your stamps. As for the thank-you notes, purchase a floral or love theme stamp.

CANCELED, POSTPONED, OR CHANGED WEDDING PLANS
Invited guests must be informed immediately by telephone or telegram, or, if

there is time, by printed card. You may need to enlist the help of friends and relatives to carry this out.

A printed card may read:

Mr. and Mrs. John Jones
announce that the marriage of
their daughter
Beverly
to
Mr. Adam Smith
will not take place
(or has been postponed)

If the date of a wedding has to be changed and the invitations have not yet been sent out, a card may be printed and enclosed stating the change. Otherwise, the old date could be crossed out and the new date inserted.

ANNOUNCEMENTS

The wedding announcement is a very favorable way of communicating with friends who live far away or who could not be invited due to a limited guest list. Announcements may also be sent to ac-

quaintances who would be interested in knowing the event had taken place.

They are not sent to anyone receiving an invitation, and do not require a gift in return.

Ideally, announcements should be ready to mail the day after the wedding. However, they may be mailed several months later. The names of the bride's parents or both sets of parents may appear on the announcement, or the couple themselves often announce their own wedding. This would be especially true in the case of a mature widow or divorcee. An "at home" card can be included.

WEDDING ANNOUNCEMENT

Doctor and Mrs. Paul Culverwell Nealy
have the honour of
announcing the marriage
of their daughter
Christine Louise
to
Mr. William Pennington
Saturday, the ninth of June
nineteen hundred and eighty-four
Lakewood, New Jersey

STATIONERY CHECKLIST				
Needed	Number	Color	Paper	Cost
Invitations				
Announcement party	————	————	————	$ ————
Rehearsal dinner	————	————	————	————
Wedding invitations				
Ceremony only	————	————	————	————
Ceremony and reception	————	————	————	————
Reception only	————	————	————	————
Informal invitations	————	————	————	————
Extra envelopes	————	————	————	————
Enclosures				
Reception cards	————	————	————	————
Response cards and envelopes	————	————	————	————
Pew cards	————	————	————	————
At home cards	————	————	————	————
Maps	————	————	————	————
Announcements	————	————	————	————
Gift acknowledgment cards	————	————	————	————
Informal thank-yous	————	————	————	————
Place cards				
Rehearsal dinner	————	————	————	————
Reception	————	————	————	————
Napkins	————	————	————	————
Postage				
Invitations	————	————	————	————
Announcements	————	————	————	————
Response envelopes	————	————	————	————
			Total	$ ————

Wedding Cake

The bride's cake is important to your wedding reception because you and your guests are drawn together as it is shared. You and your groom each take a bite of the first piece as a pledge of your willingness to share life together, and then kiss to seal this promise. The cake is then cut and served to everyone present so that they may participate in the festivities expressive of your joy.

The main purpose of a reception is to have a time when the guests may congratulate you and your groom, and then greet one another. Therefore, it isn't necessary to spend all your time and money trying to impress everyone with the most magnificent cake of the century. An attractive cake that fits the style of your wedding and is large enough for everyone to share is satisfactory.

Years ago, a wedding reception included a groom's cake. (Some ethnic groups still carry on this tradition today.) This was a dark fruitcake baked several months in advance. It was sometimes placed in an airtight box and set on top of the wedding cake to serve as the first tier—the box then being iced and decorated to match the rest of the bride's cake. When the reception was over, it was saved to be served on future anniversa-

ries. Or, more often, it was cut into little squares before the wedding and packed into small white or silver boxes, sometimes monogrammed or stamped with the bride's and groom's initials and the date. These boxes were either placed by the door, or at each person's place setting at a sit-down reception. The tradition was, then, to take the piece home and to place it under your pillow. For the newly married couple it was to bring fruitfulness. For the unmarried female it was to bring dreams of her future "Mr. Right."

If a groom's cake appears today, it is usually just a sheet cake that is of a different flavor (often chocolate). It is set on a separate table and offers the guests an alternative to the bride's cake. (It also cuts down on congestion at the main table.) The significance of the groom's cake is to serve as a reminder of the richness and fruitfulness marriage brings to our lives.

Sometimes at a reception that does not have a groom's cake, small boxes containing nuts and mints are presented to the guests instead.

SHOPPING FOR THE CAKE
Shopping for the wedding cake can be a "delicious" experience. Get recommenda-

tions of good bakeries from a recent bride or her mother; or the food editor of your local newspaper may have some suggestions. Then go to the different bakeries and view and sample their cakes. Study their sample books for shapes and colors. Make notes of your impressions, good and bad.

Perhaps you'd like to create a cake especially for you and your groom. Ray and Carolyn did this. They were from two missionary families and the mothers were able to find miniature figures and objects from the countries each of them was from. The baker, a woman who worked out of her home, made two heart-shaped layer cakes and joined them in the middle. On one was depicted a rice paddy scene; on the other, mountains and the antenna of the missionary radio station. Needless to say, everyone at the reception enjoyed viewing this personalized creation!

Here are some things to keep in mind while cake shopping:

FLAVORS
- White or yellow is traditional for the bride's cake. It should be baked no more than two days before the wedding or baked earlier and then frozen until the day before the wedding.
- Spice, chocolate, banana, carrot, German chocolate, sponge, or pound cake (These usually cost extra.)

SHAPES
- Traditional is two to five tiers, with or without pillars. Each tier is usually three layers. Remember, tiers make the cake look better and are easier to cut.
- Round tends to be most impressive
- Square

- Two hearts, wedding bells, rings, military insignia

SIZE
To determine, ask these questions:
- What is the quantity of cake to order for the number of guests?
- How large will the pieces be?
- How much do I want left over to take home?
- Can the top tier be frozen and saved for my first anniversary?
- Should I order a small cake for the wedding party and sheet cakes or petit fours for the guests? What is the most economical cake to buy?

ICING
- White is the traditional color for icing. It may have touches of pastel pink or yellow for trimmings, or pale green for leaves. If done properly, having the colors of the cake match the colors of the bridesmaids' dresses is striking. Be cautious, though, so as to prevent the colors from becoming too vivid or garish.
- A buttercream icing is delicious. Whipped cream will not hold up unless it is frosted at the site.
- Fillings of fruit or nut flavorings may be used rather than icing.

DECORATIONS
- Many types of decorations can be used. One of the more attractive ways of decorating your cake is to have fresh flowers on the top, trailing down the sides, or around the bottom of the cake.
- Small fountains or ice sculptures can be very effective.
- Bakeries have a display of decoration tops you can order.
- Ask these questions:
  If flowers are to be used to decorate the

cake, who is responsible for providing them—the florist or the bakery?

Will the bakery leave a space for a small vial of water to hold the flowers?

Is it possible to use a traditional or family heirloom for the top?

PRICE

- There are set prices for the variety of different ways that the cake can be put together. A down payment will be required at the time of ordering. Bakeries often require that the cake be paid for in full two weeks before the wedding.
- A refundable deposit is usually required for the tier supports, the cake bases, and a cake knife, if used.
- If you order a groom's cake, your baker will charge for cutting and wrapping the individual pieces. (Having friends do this can cut down on expenses here.)

DELIVERY

- Does the bakery deliver? (Is there an extra charge?) If so, they should allow enough time to assemble a large cake at the reception site. The delivery person should be equipped to repair any damage that may occur during delivery.
- If they do not deliver, arrangements should be made to move the cake in a large vehicle, such as a van.

However you find your baker, make sure you select one with a good reputation. After you've decided, use the worksheet included in this chapter to place your order, and to get in writing the cake size, flavors and fillings chosen, the color of the icing and decorations, and the top decoration. (Give one copy to the bakery and keep one yourself.)

Confirm the order by phone two days before the wedding.

WORKSHEET FOR ORDERING WEDDING CAKE

Bride _____ Phone _____

Wedding date _____

Reception site _____ Address _____

Phone _____

Time to deliver _____

Person in charge _____

Number of guests _____   *Cost*

Size of cake _____   _____

Description of shape of cake:

Flavor _____ Filling _____

Icing

     Flavor_____ Color _____ Type of decoration _____

Top of cake _____   _____

Groom's cake _____ Boxes _____ Packed _____   _____

Other bakery needs: (bread, pastries, breakfast rolls)   _____

Total cost _____   **Total $** _____

Deposit _____

(Knife, posts, etc.)

Down payment _____

Balance _____

Ceremony Specifics

There is a tendency when planning a wedding to get caught up in all of the extraneous details. But more important than how the church and/or the wedding party looks is how meaningful and worshipful the ceremony is. Take time as you read this chapter to focus on the meaning and sacredness of marriage; then concentrate on making your ceremony a reflection of that.

The church office can probably provide you with an example of a ceremony done at the church. And many of the major denominations have standard orders of service that are readily available. We have included five of these in this chapter. Glancing through one or more of these orders of service may give you workable ideas for your own ceremony.

Before talking with the minister about the wedding ceremony, you should realize that the Bible doesn't specify exactly what a wedding should include. There isn't one "right" ceremony. That is why we have such extremes within the Church itself. For instance, an old Quaker wedding simply had the bride and groom declare their love and commitment as part of the Sunday morning worship service. On the opposite extreme there were the lavish baroque marriage ceremonies of the European monarchs.

Even though the Bible doesn't give any clear-cut answers, there are some beautiful wedding traditions which have developed from the Christian context. You and your groom will be wise to attend closely to the traditions of the church to which you belong.

Be careful as you plan your ceremony. We would not encourage the use of "pop" jargon, because it might prove embarrassing as you look back on your wedding in future years. On the other hand, time-honored forms of expression will wear well with the years. This does not mean there shouldn't be any contemporary touches to your ceremony. However, such uses should be done carefully and with taste.

Do not think of your wedding as a show or performance. Your ceremony should be a time of worship as you pledge yourselves to each other and to the God who brought you together.

As you meet with the minister to discuss the wedding plans, keep in mind that there are as many opinions of what is right or wrong in a ceremony as there are ministers. And each minister will vary in flexibility. Some won't allow variations, while others will be willing to try anything. You will have some idea of what to expect if the minister who is marrying you is from your home church. Whatever your situation, do not come across as presenting your minister with orders. Be flexible yourself; be a learner.

ORDER OF SERVICE OUTLINES

Below are examples of five standard orders of service: Presbyterian, Methodist, Episcopal, Lutheran, and Baptist, followed by a service from an interdenominational church. Items listed in italics are considered optional. Though other samples could also have been included, most would be variations of one of these forms.

The complete texts of the denominational services are included at the end of this chapter.

PRESBYTERIAN ORDER OF SERVICE

Prelude
Solo (or special music)
Processional
Call to Worship
Hymn (or solo or special music)
Charge
    (Minister's introductory remarks which describe the nature of Christian marriage.)
Prayer
Declaration of Intent
    (Bride and groom signify intent by responding to the pastor's questions with a vocal affirmation. If the bride is being given away, it takes place at this time.)
Reading of Scripture
Homily (brief sermon)
Exchange of Vows ← Our hymn
Exchange of Rings
Christ Candle
    It should be noted that the Christ candle (sometimes called the unity candle) may also be placed after the pronouncement of marriage.
Prayer for the Couple (ending in the Lord's Prayer)
Hymn (or solo or special music)
Pronouncement of Marriage
Benediction
Kiss
Recessional
Postlude

METHODIST ORDER OF SERVICE

Prelude
Solo (or special music)
Processional
Call to Worship
Hymn (or solo or special music)
Charge
    (Minister's introductory remarks which describe the
    nature of Christian marriage.)
Declaration of Intent
    (Bride and groom signify their intent by responding to
    the minister's questions with a vocal affirmation. If the
    bride is being given away, it takes place at this time.)
Reading of Scripture
Homily
Exchange of Vows
Exchange of Rings
Christ Candle
Pronouncement of Marriage
Prayer for the Couple
The Lord's Prayer
Benediction
Recessional
Postlude

EPISCOPAL ORDER OF SERVICE

Prelude
Solo (or special music)
Processional
Charge
    (Minister's introductory remarks which describe the
    nature of Christian marriage.)
Declaration of Consent
    (Bride and groom signify their consent by responding to
    the minister's questions with vocal affirmation. The
    congregation also responds. If there is a giving in
    marriage, it takes place at this time.)
Hymn (or psalm or anthem)
People's Response
Prayer

Reading of Scripture
Psalm (or hymn or anthem)
People's Response
Homily (or other response to readings)
Exchange of Vows
Exchange of Rings
Pronouncement of Marriage
Prayers
     (If Communion is to follow, the Lord's Prayer may be
     omitted here.)
The Final Prayer (called "The Blessing of the Marriage")
Responsive Benediction (called "The Peace")
Kiss
Recessional
Postlude

LUTHERAN ORDER OF SERVICE

Prelude
Hymn (or solo or special music)
Processional
Call to Worship
Scripture
Homily
Hymn
Charge
     (Minister's introductory remarks which describe the
     nature of Christian marriage.)
Declaration of Intent
     (Bride and Groom signify their intent by responding to
     the minister's questions with a vocal affirmation.)
Giving of the Bride
Exchange of Vows
Exchange of Rings
Pronouncement of Marriage
Hymn (or solo or special music)
Blessing on the Couple
The Lord's Prayer
Prayer for the Couple
Hymn (or solo or special music)
Benediction
Kiss
Recessional
Postlude

BAPTIST ORDER OF SERVICE

Prelude
Hymn (or solo or special music)
Processional
Charge
    (Minister's introductory remarks which describe the
    nature of Christian marriage.)
Giving of the Bride
Homily
Prayer
Hymn (or solo or special music)
Exchange of Vows
Exchange of Rings
Scripture (Ruth 1:16)
Pronouncement of Marriage
Prayer
The Lord's Prayer
Hymn (or solo or special music)
Benediction
Kiss
Recessional
Postlude

INTERDENOMINATIONAL ORDER OF SERVICE

Of course, there are hundreds of variations possible.
Included here is one example to suggest some of the options.
A service that ties the other five together can be very
beautiful.

The text for this service is included along with the other
texts at the end of the chapter.

Prelude
Solo (or special music)
Processional
Presentation of the Bride
Call to Worship
Charge
    (Minister's introductory remarks which describe the
    nature of Christian marriage.)
Prayer
Hymn
Reading of Scripture

Homily
Exchange of Vows
Exchange of Rings
Prayer
Pronouncement of Marriage
Christ Candle
Vows of the Christian Home
Prayer for the Couple
Solo (or special music)
Kiss
Presentation
Recessional
Postlude

VARIATIONS

There are seven areas of the wedding service in which your pastor may possibly allow some changes. They are listed below along with several options. When considering these options, make sure your selection reflects your personal worship and commitment. Don't add something just because it's new and unusual.

Words to be verbalized by the bride and groom or the guests are in italics.

The Call to Worship

✓*Option A* Our Lord Jesus said: From the beginning of creation, God made them male and female. For this reason, a man shall leave his father and mother and be joined to his wife, so they are no longer two but one. Let us worship God.

Option B We are gathered here to worship God and to witness the marriage vows of _____ and _____ [full names]. Let your light so shine before people that they may see your good works and give glory to your Father who is in heaven. Let us worship God.

Option C Beloved, let us love one another, for love is of God, and he who loves is born of God and knows God. Let us worship God.

Option D Let us join in celebration. We have been invited to share the joy of this day with _____ and _____. We are their family and friends, and together we form a community to worship God and to witness their wedding. Let us worship.

Option E Except the Lord build the house, they that build it labor in vain. Our help is in the name of the Lord, who made heaven and earth. Let us worship God.

Option F _____ and _____ greet you. It is their desire that you enter into the joy and beauty and reverence of the following moments. Let us worship God.

The Charge

Option A _____ and _____, marriage is an honorable estate whose bond and covenant was instituted by God in creation. Our Lord Jesus Christ adorned and beautified this holy estate by His presence and first miracle at a wedding in Cana of Galilee. It signifies to us the mystery of the union between Christ and His Church. And the Holy Scripture commends it to be honored among all people.

Therefore no one should enter this state of life unadvisedly, lightly, or wantonly; but reverently, discreetly, advisedly, soberly, and in the fear of God; duly considering the causes for which matrimony was ordained.

Option B Dearly beloved, we are assembled here in the presence of God, to join this man and this woman in holy marriage; which is instituted of God, regulated by His commandments, blessed by our Lord Jesus Christ, and to be held in honor among all men. Let us therefore reverently remember that God has established and sanctified marriage for the welfare and happiness of mankind. Our Savior has declared that a man shall forsake his father and mother and cleave unto his wife. By His apostles, He has instructed those who enter into this relation to cherish a mutual esteem and love; to bear with each other's infirmities and weaknesses; to comfort each other in sickness, trouble, and sorrow; in honor and industry to provide for each other and for their household in temporal things; to pray for and encourage each other in the things which pertain to God; and to live together as heirs of the grace of life.

Option C Today you are presenting yourselves before this congregation to declare your intention of uniting your lives voluntarily and honorably for the service of God and man. You are making a double dedication: to each other, in a lasting and indivisible union that shall endure for the remaining years of your lives; and to God, that He may make you His dual instru-

ment for the accomplishment of His purpose both in and by your personalities. The achievement of this purpose will require appreciation of each other's abilities and virtues, forgiveness of each other's faults, and unfailing devotion to each other's welfare and development. There must be on your part a united consent to the purpose of God as He progressively reveals it to you by His Word and by His Spirit, and an unhesitant acceptance by faith of the challenges that He sets before you.

I charge you, therefore, first of all, to consider that your promises to each other are made in the presence of a God who remembers your pledges and who holds you responsible for performing them. They must be kept inviolable before Him.

I admonish you to keep in mind that each of you is the object of Christ's redemption, and should be valued accordingly. Neither should be neglected or belittled by the other. Esteem each other as God's gift for mutual aid, comfort, and joy, and as a repository of complete confidence and trust.

I encourage you to share willingly and sympathetically your joys and worries, your successes and your struggles, and to be neither conceited by the former nor depressed by the latter. Whichever may prevail, cling closely to each other, that defeats may be met by a united strength, and victories by a united joy.

I charge you to make your home a place where you will have a refuge from the storms of life, not only for yourselves, but also for others who may be your guests. Let it be a haven for the weary, a source of uplift for the discouraged, and a convincing testimony to a cynical world.

In short, recognize the Lord Jesus Christ as the head of the house, the ruler of your

lives)
~~destinies~~, and the object of your deepest affection. If you do, He will confirm your marriage by His guidance and will overshadow it with His peace. I charge you to love each other, to support each other, and to serve Him with sincere hearts and determined wills until your mutual service for Him shall be completed.

The Declaration of Intent
In the following examples, (G) signifies groom, (B) signifies bride, and (P) signifies parents.

Option A (G)_____ , wilt thou have this woman to be thy wedded wife, to live together after God's ordinance in the holy estate of matrimony? Wilt thou love her, comfort her, honor and keep her in sickness and in health; and forsaking all others, keep thee only unto her, so long as ye both shall live?
(G) *I will.*
(B)_____ , wilt thou have this man to be thy wedded husband, to live together after God's ordinance in the holy estate of matrimony? Wilt thou love him, comfort him, honor and keep him in sickness and in health; and forsaking all others, keep thee only unto him, so long as ye both shall live?
(B) *I will.*

Option B (G)_____ , will you have this woman to be your wife, to live together in holy marriage? Will you love her, comfort her, honor and keep her, in sickness and in health, and forsaking all others, be faithful to her as long as you both shall live?
(G) *I will.*
(B)_____ , will you have this man to be your husband, to live together in holy marriage? Will you love him, com-fort him, honor and keep him, in sickness and in health, and forsaking all others, be faithful to him as long as you both shall live?
(B) *I will.*

Option C (G)_____ , will you have this woman to be your wife, and will you pledge yourself to her in all love and honor, in all duty and service, in all faith and tenderness, to live with her and cherish her, according to the ordinance of God, in the holy bond of marriage?
(G) *I will.*
(B)_____ , will you have this man to be your husband, and will you pledge yourself to him in all love and honor, in all duty and service, in all faith and tenderness, to live with him and cherish him, according to the ordinance of God, in the holy bond of marriage?
(B) *I will.*

Option D (The minister will address first the man, then the woman, and finally the parents of both.)
(G)_____ , do you desire to be united in marriage with (B)_____ , and will you love her, comfort her, honor her and be her helper, as long as you both shall live?
(G) *I do and I will.*
(B)_____ , do you desire to be united in marriage with (G)_____ , and will you love him, comfort him, honor him and be his helper, as long as you both shall live?
(B) *I do and I will.*
(The parents of the bride and groom will stand.)
Will you the parents of _____ and _____ do all in your power to uphold their marriage in the years ahead, and will you promise to pray for and encourage them, that they may fulfill the

vows they are making today?

(P) *We will.*

✓*Option E* (G)_____ , will you take (B)_____ to be your wife, and will you be faithful to her, love her, honor her, live with her and cherish her, according to the commandments of God in holy marriage?

(G) *I will.*

(B)_____ , will you take (G) _____ to be your husband, and will you be faithful to him, love him, honor him, live with him and cherish him, according to the commandments of God in holy marriage?

(B) *I will.*

✓*Option F* Christian marriage is most serious, because it will bind you together for life in a relationship so close and so intimate that the two of you will become one. Before you lies a future with its hopes and disappointments, its successes and its failures, its pleasures and its pains, its joys and its sorrows. These elements are mingled in every life and are to be expected, but for Christians they are not there to be received with resignation, but with hope and joy and all the spiritual gifts God's Spirit promises us.

(G)_____ , do you come here freely to take (B)_____ as your wife, according to the commandments of God in holy marriage?

(G) *I do.*

(B)_____ , do you come here freely to take (G)_____ as your husband, according to the commandments of God in holy marriage?

(B) *I do.*

Option G (G)_____ , do you take (B)_____ to be your wife, to live together in the holy bond of married life?

Do you promise to honor and uphold her, and to join with her in making a home that shall endure in love and peace? Do you affirm your purpose of a deeper union with her, whereby you both shall know joy and fulfillment of love? Do you pledge to her your complete faithfulness through all the changing experiences of life? And, of your own free volition, do you now give yourself to her completely (body, mind, and soul) that from this day forth you shall be hers alone, so long as you both live?

(G) *I do.*

(B)_____ , do you take (G) _____ to be your husband, to live together in the holy bond of married life? Do you promise to honor and uphold him, and to join with him in making a home that shall endure in love and peace? Do you affirm your purpose of a deeper union with him, whereby you both shall know joy and fulfillment of love? Do you pledge to him your complete faithfulness through all the changing experiences of life? And, of your own free volition, do you now give yourself to him completely (body, mind, and soul) that from this day forth you shall be his alone, so long as you both live?

(B) *I do.*

The Reading of Scripture

Any of the following passages is appropriate for a wedding service: Genesis 2:18-24; Ecclesiastes 4:9-12; Matthew 5:13-16; John 2:1; Ephesians 5:21-33; Colossians 3:12-17; 1 John 4:7-12. *N.b.*

The Exchange of Vows

Some couples write their own vows—an exercise we would advise against. However, if you *are* determined to do so, take great care; don't make them any longer than the normal vows, and don't be overly sentimental or clever. Lance Morrow, in an editorial essay for *Time* magazine entitled "The Hazards of Homemade Vows" (June 1983), warns: "Some couples remain tempted today by the opportunity a wedding offers for self-expression. It is a temptation that should be resisted. The vows that couples devise are, with some exceptions, never as moving to the guests as they are to the couple. . . .

"If the bride and groom have intimacies to whisper, there are private places for that. A wedding is public business. That is the point of it. The couple are not merely marrying one another. They are, at least in part, submitting themselves to the larger logics of life, to the survival of the community, to life itself. . . . At the moment of their binding, they should subsume their egos into that larger business within which their small lyricisms become tinny and exhibitionistic."

Also, although it is nice to have your vows memorized, it is not advisable to try to say them from memory. The stress of the wedding day is enough without this added pressure.

Option A *I (G)_____ take thee (B) _____ to be my wedded wife, to have and to hold from this day forward, for better for worse, for richer for poorer, in sickness and in health, to love and to cherish, till death do us part.*

I (B)_____ take thee (G) _____ to be my wedded husband, to have and to hold from this day forward, for better for worse, for richer for poorer, in sickness and in health, to love and to cherish, till death do us part.

Option B *I (G)_____ take you (B) _____ to be my wife, to have and to hold from this day forward, for better for worse, for richer for poorer, in sickness and in health, to love and to cherish, until we are parted by death. This is my solemn vow.*

I (B)_____ take you (G) _____ to be my husband, to have and to hold from this day forward, for better for worse, for richer for poorer, in sickness and in health, to love and to cherish, until we are parted by death. This is my solemn vow.

Option C *I (G)_____ take thee (B) _____ to be my wedded wife, and I do promise and covenant before God and these witnesses, to be thy loving and faithful husband, in plenty and in want, in joy and in sorrow, in sickness and in health, as long as we both shall live.*

I (B)_____ take thee (G) _____ to be my wedded husband, and I do promise and covenant before God and these witnesses, to be thy loving and faithful wife, in plenty and in want, in joy and in sorrow, in sickness and in health, as long as we both shall live.

Option D *(B)_____, I promise with God's help to be your faithful husband, to love and serve you as Christ commands, as long as we both shall live.*

(G)_____, I promise with God's help to be your faithful wife, to love and serve you as Christ commands, as long as we both shall live.

Option E *(B)_____, I promise before God, our family, and friends, to be your loving and faithful husband, to share my life with you, in wealth and in poverty, in sickness and in health, in good times and in bad times, for as long as we both shall live.*

(G)_____, I promise before God, our family, and friends, to be your loving

and faithful wife, to share my life with you, in wealth and in poverty, in sickness and in health, in good times and in bad times, for as long as we both shall live.

Option F I (G)_____ take you (B) _____ to be my wife, and I promise before God and these friends, that I will share my life with you in all love and honor, in all faith and tenderness, through joy and sorrow, in sickness and health, as long as we both shall live.

I (B)_____ take you (G) _____ to be my husband, and I promise before God and these friends, that I will share my life with you in all love and honor, in all faith and tenderness, through joy and sorrow, in sickness and health, as long as we both shall live.

Option G I (G)_____ take you (B) _____ to be my wife. I promise to be true to you in good times and in bad, in sickness and in health. I will love you and honor you all the days of my life.

I (B)_____ take you (G) _____ to be my husband. I promise to be true to you in good times and in bad, in sickness and in health. I will love you and honor you all the days of my life.

Option H (Said by both.) I draw you into my very being to share with you life's sorrows and joys. I promise to respect you and be respected by you, to forgive you and be forgiven by you, to instill hope in you and be given hope by you. I promise to accept the mystery of your uniqueness and to love you as an equal. Through these acts of teaching and learning, we will grow toward each other.

Exchange of Rings

Option A Bless, O Lord, this ring, that he (she) who gives it and she (he) who wears it may abide in thy peace, and continue in thy favor, unto their life's end, through Jesus Christ our Lord. Amen.

(Said by both.) *With this ring I thee wed, in the name of the Father, and of the Son, and of the Holy Ghost. Amen.*

Option B Eternal God, we pray for your blessing upon these rings that they may be a permanent reminder of holy promises and steadfast love. Bless those who wear them that they may remain in your favor throughout all their earthly life, through Jesus Christ our Lord. Amen.

(Said by both.) *This ring is the sign of my promise, and I give it to you in the name of the Father, and of the Son, and of the Holy Spirit. Amen.*

✓*Option C* Eternal God, bless these rings that as _____ and _____ wear them they will be reminded of their faith in you and their promises to each other. Let these rings be symbols of a deep and an unending love, through Jesus Christ our Lord. Amen.

(B)_____ , *this ring is the sign of my love and faithfulness, and I give it to you in the name of the Father, the Son, and the Holy Spirit. Amen.*

(G)_____ , *this ring is the sign of my love and faithfulness, and I give it to you in the name of the Father, the Son, and the Holy Spirit. Amen.*

Option D What symbols do you give of these holy promises?

(Said by both.) *This ring. Receive this ring as an outward pledge and symbol of my promise to fulfill these vows which we have taken.*

Option E What token do you give of your love?

(Said by both.) *A ring. With this ring I thee wed, with my body I thee worship,*

CEREMONY PLANNING SHEET

Date _____ Church _____

Officiating Clergyman _____ Phone _____

Assisting Clergyman _____ Phone _____

Call to Worship

Charge

Declaration of Intent

Reading of Scripture

Exchange of Vows

Exchange of Rings

Optional:
Christ Candle

Vows of the Christian Home

Kiss   Presentation

and with all my worldly goods I thee endow; in the name of the Father, and of the Son, and of the Holy Spirit. Amen.

Prayer: Bless, O Lord, these rings to be a symbol of the solemn vows by which this man and this woman have bound themselves to each other in holy matrimony; through Jesus Christ our Lord. Amen.

The Christ Candle

Most churches provide a special Christ candle (or unity candle) candelabra that holds three candles. Usually, when the wedding candles are lighted, the two outside candles are lit, leaving the center candle untouched. The two burning candles symbolize the bride and groom. When the bride and groom use these candles to light the center candle together, it symbolizes the union of their lives in Christ.

It may be lit without an introduction, or after the minister's remarks (see interdenominational service text).

Vows of the Christian Home

Realizing the weakening structure of the family in society today, many Christian couples are interested in more than pledging themselves to one another; they desire to establish nurturing homes in which to build Christians. To this end, during the ceremony, the wedded couple repeats the following vows together:

Depending upon God for strength and wisdom, we pledge ourselves to the establishment of a Christian home. Together we will constantly seek God's will and honor Christ in our marriage.

TEXTS OF WEDDING CEREMONIES

As you examine the five sample denominational wedding texts, you should remember that they do not mention the prelude, processional, recessional, or postlude. Neither do they consistently include the homily (short sermon) or suggestions as to where special music, hymns, or the Christ candle might be placed. However, if they are read with reference to the sample orders given earlier in this chapter, they are easily understandable.

PRESBYTERIAN

(Call to Worship)

Dearly beloved, we are assembled here in the presence of God, to join this man and this woman in holy marriage; which is instituted of God, regulated by His commandments, blessed by our Lord Jesus Christ, and to be held in honor among all men. Let us therefore reverently remember that God has established and sanctified marriage, for the welfare and happiness of mankind. Our Savior has declared that a man shall leave his father and mother and cleave unto his wife. By His apostles, He has instructed those who enter into this relation to cherish a mutual esteem and love; to bear with each other's infirmities and weaknesses; to comfort each other in sickness, trouble, and sorrow; in honesty and industry to provide for each other, and for their household, in temporal things; to pray for and encourage each other in the things which pertain to God; and to live together as the heirs of the grace of life.

Forasmuch as these two persons have come hither to be made one in this holy estate, if there be any here present who knows any just cause why they may not lawfully be joined in marriage, I require him now to make it known, or ever after to hold his peace.
(Charge)

I charge you both, before the great God, the Searcher of all hearts, that if either of you know any reason why ye may not lawfully be joined together in marriage, ye do now confess it. For be ye well assured that if any persons are joined together otherwise than as God's Word allows, their union is not blessed by Him.
(Prayer)

Almighty and ever-blessed God, whose presence is the happiness of every condition, and whose favor hallows every relation: We beseech Thee to be present and favorable unto these Thy servants, that they may be truly joined in the honorable estate of marriage, in the covenant of their God. As Thou hast brought them together by Thy providence, sanctify them by Thy Spirit, giving them a new frame of heart fit for their new estate; and enrich them with all grace, whereby they may enjoy the comforts, undergo the cares, endure the trials, and perform the duties of life together as becometh Christians, under Thy heavenly guidance and protection; through our Lord Jesus Christ. Amen.
(Declaration of Intent)

(G)_____ , wilt thou have this woman to be thy wife, and wilt thou pledge thy troth to her, in all love and honor, in all duty and service, in all faith and tenderness, to live with her and cherish her, according to the ordinance of God, in the holy bond of marriage?

(G) *I will.*

(B)_____ , wilt thou have this man to be thy husband, and wilt thou pledge thy troth to him, in all love and honor, in all duty and service, in all faith and tenderness, to live with him and cherish him, according to the ordinance of God, in the holy bond of marriage?

(B) *I will.*
(Giving of the Bride)
   Who giveth this woman to be married to this man?
(Vows)
   I (G)_____ take thee (B)_____ to be my
wedded wife. And I do promise and covenant, before God
and these witnesses, to be thy loving and faithful husband,
in plenty and in want, in joy and in sorrow, in sickness and
in health, as long as we both shall live.
   I (B)_____ take thee (G)_____ to be my
wedded husband. And I do promise and covenant, before God
and these witnesses, to be thy loving and faithful wife, in
plenty and in want, in joy and in sorrow, in sickness and in
health, as long as we both shall live.
   (Before giving the ring, the minister may say:)
   Bless, O Lord, this ring, that he who gives it and she who
wears it may abide in Thy peace, and continue in Thy favor,
unto their life's end; through Jesus Christ our Lord. Amen.
(Exchange of rings)
   (Said by both.) *This ring I give thee, in token and pledge, of
our constant faith, and abiding love.*
                              (or)
   *With this ring I thee wed; in the name of the Father, and of
the Son, and of the Holy Spirit. Amen.*
(Prayer)
   Most merciful and gracious God, of whom the whole
family in heaven and earth is named; bestow upon these Thy
servants the seal of Thine approval, and Thy fatherly
benediction; granting unto them grace to fulfill, with pure
and steadfast affection, the vow and covenant between them
made. Guide them together, we beseech Thee, in the way of
righteousness and peace, that, loving and serving Thee, with
one heart and mind, all the days of their life, they may be
abundantly enriched with the tokens of Thine everlasting
favor, in Jesus Christ our Lord. Amen.
(The Lord's Prayer)
   *Our Father, who art in heaven, hallowed be Thy name. Thy
kingdom come. Thy will be done; on earth as it is in heaven.
Give us this day our daily bread. And forgive us our debts, as
we forgive our debtors. And lead us not into temptation, but
deliver us from evil, for thine is the kingdom, and the power,
and the glory, for ever. Amen.*
(Pronouncement of Marriage)
   By the authority committed unto me as a minister of the

Church of Christ, I declare that _____ and _____ are now husband and wife, according to the ordinance of God, and the law of the state; in the name of the Father, and of the Son, and of the Holy Spirit. Amen.

Whom therefore God hath joined together, let no man put asunder.

(Benediction)

The Lord bless you, and keep you; the Lord make His face to shine upon you, and be gracious unto you; the Lord lift up His countenance upon you, and give you peace; both now and in the life everlasting. Amen.

or

God the Father, God the Son, God the Holy Spirit, bless, preserve, and keep you; the Lord mercifully with His favor look upon you, and fill you with all spiritual benediction and grace; that ye may so live together in this life that in the world to come ye may have life everlasting. Amen.

Adapted from the *Book of Common Worship.* © 1978 by the Board of Christian Education of the United Presbyterian Church in U.S.A. Westminster Press, Philadelphia.

METHODIST

(Call to Worship)

Dearly beloved, we are gathered together here in the sight of God, and in the presence of these witnesses, to join together this man and this woman in holy matrimony; which is an honorable estate, instituted of God, and signifying unto us the mystical union which exists between Christ and His Church; which holy estate Christ adorned and beautified with His presence in Cana of Galilee. It is therefore not to be entered into unadvisedly, but reverently, discreetly, and in the fear of God. Into this holy estate these two persons come now to be joined. If any here can show just cause why they may not lawfully be joined together, let them now speak, or else hereafter forever hold their peace.

(Charge)

I require and charge you both, as you stand in the presence of God, before whom the secrets of all hearts are disclosed, that, having duly considered the holy covenant you are about to make, you do now declare before this company your pledge of faith, each to the other. Be well assured that if these solemn vows are kept inviolate, as God's Word demands, and if steadfastly you endeavor to do the will of your heavenly Father, God will bless your marriage, will grant you fulfillment in it, and will establish your home in peace.

(Declaration of Intent)

(G)_____ , wilt thou have this woman to be thy wedded wife, to live together in the holy estate of matrimony? Wilt thou love her, comfort her, honor and keep her, in sickness and in health; and forsaking all other keep thee only unto her so long as ye both shall live?

(G) *I will.*

(B)_____ , wilt thou have this man to be thy wedded husband, to live together in the holy estate of matrimony? Wilt thou love him, comfort him, honor and keep him, in sickness and in health; and forsaking all other keep thee only unto him so long as ye both shall live?

(B) *I will.*

(Bride Given Away)

Who giveth this woman to be married to this man?

(Exchange of Vows)

I (G)_____ take thee (B)_____ to be my wedded wife, to have and to hold, from this day forward, for better for worse, for richer for poorer, in sickness and in health, to love and to cherish, till death us do part, according to God's holy ordinance; and thereto I pledge thee my faith.

I (B)_____ take thee (G)_____ to be my wedded husband, to have and to hold, from this day forward, for better for worse, for richer for poorer, in sickness and in health, to love and to cherish, till death us do part, according to God's holy ordinance; and thereto I pledge thee my faith.

(Exchange of Rings)

The wedding ring is the outward and visible sign of an inward and spiritual grace, signifying to all the uniting of this man and this woman in holy matrimony, through the Church of Jesus Christ our Lord.

Let us pray. Bless, O Lord, the giving of these rings, that they who wear them may abide in Thy peace, and continue in Thy favor; through Jesus Christ our Lord. Amen.

or

Bless, O Lord, the giving of this ring, that he who gives it and she who wears it may abide forever in Thy peace, and continue in thy favor; through Jesus Christ our Lord. Amen.

(Said by both if a two-ring ceremony.) *In token and pledge of our constant faith and abiding love, with this ring I thee wed, in the name of the Father, and of the Son, and of the Holy Spirit. Amen.*

(Pronouncement of Marriage)

Forasmuch as _____ and _____ have consented together in holy wedlock, and have witnessed the same before God and this company, and thereto have pledged their faith each to the other and have declared the same by joining hands and by giving and receiving rings; I pronounce that they are husband and wife together, in the name of the Father, and of the Son, and of the Holy Spirit. Those whom God hath joined together let no one put asunder. Amen.

(Prayer)

Let us pray.

O eternal God, Creator and Preserver of all mankind, Giver of all spiritual grace, the Author of everlasting life; send Thy blessing upon this man and this woman, whom we bless in Thy name, that they may surely perform and keep the vow and covenant between them made, and may ever remain in perfect love and peace together, and live according to Thy laws.

Look graciously upon them, that they may love, honor, and cherish each other, and so live together in faithfulness and patience, in wisdom and true godliness, that their home may be a haven of blessing and a place of peace; through Jesus Christ our Lord. Amen.

(The Lord's Prayer)

Our Father, who art in heaven, hallowed be Thy name. Thy kingdom come; Thy will be done, on earth as it is in heaven. Give us this day our daily bread. And forgive us our trespasses, as we forgive those who trespass against us. And lead us not into temptation, but deliver us from evil. For Thine is the kingdom, and the power, and the glory, forever. Amen.

(Benediction)

God, the Father, the Son, and the Holy Spirit, bless, preserve, and keep you; the Lord graciously with His favor look upon you, and so fill you with all spiritual benediction and love that you may so live together in this life that in the world to come you may have life everlasting. Amen.

Adapted from *The Book of Worship for Church and Home* ©1964, 1965 by the Board of Publication of the Methodist Church, Inc. Used by permission.

EPISCOPAL

(Charge)

Dearly beloved: We have come together in the presence of God to witness and bless the joining together of this man and this woman in holy matrimony. The bond and covenant of marriage was established by God in creation, and our Lord Jesus Christ adorned this manner of life by His presence and first miracle at a wedding in Cana of Galilee. It signifies to us the mystery of the union between Christ and His Church, and holy Scripture commends it to be honored among all people.

The union of husband and wife in heart, body, and mind is intended by God for their mutual joy; for the help and comfort given one another in prosperity and adversity; and, when it is God's will, for the procreation of children and their nurture in the knowledge and love of the Lord. Therefore marriage is not to be entered into unadvisedly or lightly, but reverently, deliberately, and in accordance with the purposes for which it was instituted by God.

Into this holy union ——————— and ——————— now come to be joined. If any of you can show just cause why they may not lawfully be married, speak now; or else forever hold your peace.

I require and charge you both, here in the presence of God, that if either of you know any reason why you may not be united in marriage lawfully, and in accordance with God's Word, you do now confess it.

(Declaration of Consent)

(B)———————, will you have this man to be your husband; to live together in the covenant of marriage? Will you love him, comfort him, honor and keep him, in sickness and in health; and, forsaking all others, be faithful to him as long as you both shall live?

(B) *I will.*

(G)———————, will you have this woman to be your wife; to live together in the covenant of marriage? Will you love her, comfort her, honor and keep her, in sickness and in health; and, forsaking all others, be faithful to her as long as you both shall live?

(G) *I will.*

(People's Response)

Will all of you witnessing these promises do all in your power to uphold these two persons in their marriage?

People: *We will.*
Minister: The Lord be with you.
People: *And also with you.*
(Prayer)
   Let us pray.

   O gracious and everliving God, You have created us male and female in Your image. Look mercifully upon this man and this woman who come to You seeking Your blessing, and assist them with Your grace, that with true fidelity and steadfast love they may honor and keep the promises and vows they make; through Jesus Christ our Savior, who lives and reigns with You in the unity of the Holy Spirit, one God, for ever and ever. Amen.

(Reading of Scripture)
   Genesis 1:26-28 (Male and female He created them.)
   Genesis 2:4-9, 15-24 (A man cleaves to his wife and they become one flesh.)
   Song of Solomon 2:10-13; 8:6, 7 (Many waters cannot quench love.)
   Tobit 8:5b-8 *(New English Bible)* (That she and I may grow old together.)
   1 Corinthians 13:1-13 (Love is patient and kind.)
   Ephesians 3:14-19 (The Father from whom every family is named.)
   Ephesians 5:1, 2, 21-33 (Walk in love, as Christ loved us.)
   Colossians 3:12-17 (Love which binds everything together in harmony.)
   1 John 4:7-16 (Let us love one another for love is of God.)
(Hymn)
(People's Response)
Minister: The holy gospel of our Lord Jesus Christ according to _____
People: *Glory to you, Lord Christ.*
   Matthew 5:1-10 (The Beatitudes.)
   Matthew 5:13-16 (You are the light . . . let your light so shine.)
   Matthew 7:21, 24-29 (Like a wise man who built his house upon the rock.)
   Mark 10:6-9, 13-16 (They are no longer two but one.)
   John 15:9-12 (Love one another as I have loved you.)
Minister: The gospel of the Lord.
People: *Praise to you, Lord Christ.*
(Exchange of Vows)
   In the name of God, I (G)_____ take you

(B)_____ to be my wife, to have and to hold from this day forward, for better for worse, for richer for poorer, in sickness and in health, to love and to cherish, until we are parted by death. This is my solemn vow.

In the name of God, I (B)_____ take you (G)_____ to be my husband, to have and to hold from this day forward, for better for worse, for richer for poorer, in sickness and in health, to love and to cherish, until we are parted by death. This is my solemn vow.

(Exchange of Rings)

Bless, O Lord, this ring to be a sign of the vows by which this man and this woman have bound themselves to each other; through Jesus Christ our Lord. Amen.

(Said by both if a two-ring ceremony.) _____ , *I give you this ring as a symbol of my vow, and with all that I am and all that I have, I honor you, in the name of the Father, and of the Son, and of the Holy Spirit (or in the name of God).*

(Pronouncement of Marriage)

Now that _____ and _____ have given themselves to each other by solemn vows, with the joining of hands and the giving and receiving of a ring, I pronounce that they are husband and wife, in the name of the Father, and of the Son, and of the Holy Spirit.

Those whom God has joined together let no one put asunder.

People: *Amen.*

(Prayers)

Let us pray together in the words our Savior taught us. *Our Father, who art in heaven, hallowed be Thy name. Thy kingdom come; Thy will be done, on earth as it is in heaven. Give us this day our daily bread. And forgive us our trespasses, as we forgive those who trespass against us. And lead us not into temptation, but deliver us from evil. For Thine is the kingdom, and the power, and the glory, for ever and ever. Amen.*

or

Our Father in heaven, hallowed be Your name. Your kingdom come; Your will be done, on earth as in heaven. Give us today our daily bread. Forgive us our sins as we forgive those who sin against us. Save us from the time of trial, and deliver us from evil. For the kingdom, the power, and the glory are Yours, now and for ever. Amen.

Let us pray.

Eternal God, Creator and Preserver of all life, Author of salvation, and Giver of all grace; look with favor upon the world You have made, and for which Your Son gave His life, and especially upon this man and this woman whom You make one flesh in holy matrimony. Amen.

Give them wisdom and devotion in the ordering of their common life, that each may be to the other a strength in need, a counselor in perplexity, a comfort in sorrow, and a companion in joy. Amen.

Grant that their wills may be so knit together in Your will, and their spirits in Your Spirit, that they may grow in love and peace with You and one another all the days of their life. Amen.

Give them grace, when they hurt each other, to recognize and acknowledge their fault, and to seek each other's forgiveness and Yours. Amen.

Make their life together a sign of Christ's love to this sinful and broken world, that unity may overcome estrangement, forgiveness heal guilt, and joy conquer despair. Amen.

Bestow on them, if it is Your will, the gift and heritage of children, and the grace to bring them up to know You, to love You, and to serve You. Amen.

Give them such fulfillment of their mutual affection that they may reach out in love and concern for others. Amen.

Grant that all married persons who have witnessed these vows may find their lives strengthened and their loyalties confirmed. Amen.

Grant that the bonds of our common humanity, by which all Your children are united one to another, and the living to the dead, may be so transformed by Your grace, that Your will may be done on earth as it is in heaven; where, O Father, with Your Son and the Holy Spirit, You live and reign in perfect unity, now and for ever. Amen.

Most gracious God, we give You thanks for Your tender love in sending Jesus Christ to come among us, to be born of a human mother, and to make the way of the cross to be the way of life. We thank You, also, for consecrating the union of man and woman in His name. By the power of Your Holy Spirit, pour out the abundance of Your blessing upon this man and this woman. Defend them from every enemy. Lead them into all peace. Let their love for each other be a seal upon their hearts, a mantle about their shoulders, and a crown upon their foreheads. Bless them in their work and in their companionship; in their sleeping and in their waking; in their joys and in their sorrows; in their life and in their death. Finally, in Your mercy, bring them to that table where your saints feast for ever in your heavenly home; through Jesus Christ our Lord, who with You and the Holy Spirit lives and reigns, one God, for ever and ever. Amen.

or

O God, You have so consecrated the covenant of marriage that in it is represented the spiritual unity between Christ and His Church. Send therefore Your blessing upon these Your servants, that they may so love, honor, and cherish each other in faithfulness and patience, in wisdom and true godliness, that their home may be a haven of blessing and peace; through Jesus Christ our Lord, who lives and reigns with You and the Holy Spirit, one God, now and for ever. Amen.

(The final prayer)

God the Father, God the Son, God the Holy Spirit, bless, preserve, and keep you; the Lord mercifully with His favor look upon you, and fill you with all spiritual benediction and grace; that you may faithfully live together in this life, and in the age to come have life everlasting. Amen.

(Responsive benediction)

Minister: The peace of the Lord be always with you.

People: *And also with you.*

Adapted from *The Book of Common Prayer,* Kingsport Press, Kingsport, Tennessee, 1977, revision of *The Book of Common Prayer,* 1928.

BAPTIST

(Charge)

Dear friends (or dearly beloved, or beloved friends), we are here assembled in the presence of God to unite _____ and _____ in marriage.

The Bible teaches that marriage is to be a permanent relationship of one man and one woman freely and totally committed to each other as companions for life. Our Lord declared that man shall leave his father and mother and unite with his wife in the building of a home, and the two shall become one flesh.

(Bride given away)

Who gives the bride to be married?

(Homily)

The home is built upon love, which virtue is best portrayed in the thirteenth chapter of Paul's first letter to the Corinthians. "Love is patient and kind; love is not jealous or boastful; it is not arrogant or rude. Love does not insist on its own way; it is not irritable or resentful; it does not rejoice at wrong, but rejoices in the right. Love bears all things, believes all things, hopes all things, endures all things. Love never ends; . . . So faith, hope, love abide, these three; but the greatest of these is love" (1 Cor. 13:4-13, RSV).

Marriage is a companionship which involves mutual commitment and responsibility. You will share alike in the responsibilities and the joys of life. When companions share a sorrow the sorrow is halved, and when they share a joy the joy is doubled.

You are exhorted to dedicate your home to your Creator. Take His Word, the Bible, for your guide. Give loyal devotion to His church, thus uniting the mutual strength of these two most important institutions, living your lives as His willing servants, and true happiness will be your temporal and eternal reward.

(Prayer)

Let us pray. O Lord of life and love, bestow Thy grace upon this marriage, and seal this commitment of Thy children with Thy love.

As Thou hast brought them together by Thy divine providence, sanctify them by Thy Spirit, that they may give themselves fully one to the other and to Thee. Give them strength and patience to live their lives in a manner that will mutually bless themselves and honor Thy holy name; through Jesus Christ our Lord. Amen.

(Exchange of Vows)

(G)_____ , will you take (B)_____ to be your wife; will you commit yourself to her happiness and her self-fulfillment as a person, and to her usefulness in God's kingdom; and will you promise to love, honor, trust, and serve her in sickness and in health, in adversity and prosperity, and to be true and loyal to her, so long as you both shall live?

(G) *I will.*

(B)_____ , will you take (G)_____ to be your husband; will you commit yourself to his happiness and his self-fulfillment as a person, and to his usefulness in God's kingdom; and will you promise to love, honor, trust, and serve him in sickness and in health, in adversity and prosperity, and to be true and loyal to him, so long as you both shall live?

(B) *I will.*

(Exchange of Rings)

The wedding ring is a symbol of marriage in at least two ways: the purity of gold symbolizes the purity of your love for each other, and the unending circle symbolizes the unending vows which you are taking, which may be broken honorably in the sight of God only by death. As a token of your vows, you will give and receive the rings (or ring).

(G)_____ , you will give the ring and repeat after me: *(B)_____ , with this ring I pledge my life and love to you, in the name of the Father, and of the Son, and of the Holy Spirit.*

(B)_____ , you will give the ring and repeat after me: *(G)_____ , with this ring I pledge my love and life to you, in the name of the Father, and of the Son, and of the Holy Spirit.*

(In the case of a single ring ceremony, the bride will say, *(G)_____ , I accept this ring and pledge to you my love and life, in the name of the Father, and of the Son, and of the Holy Spirit.)*

(Scripture)

Will both of you please repeat after me:

> *Entreat me not to leave you*
> *or to return from following you;*
> *for where you go I will go,*
> *and where you lodge I will lodge;*
> *your people shall be my people,*
> *and your God my God* (Ruth 1:16, RSV).

(Pronouncement of Marriage)

Since they have made these commitments before God and this assembly (or, these witnesses), by the authority of God and the laws of this state, I declare that _____ and _____ are husband and wife.

_____ and _____ , you are no longer two independent persons but one. "What therefore God has joined together, let no man separate" (Matt. 19:6, NASB).

(Prayer)

(The Lord's Prayer)

Our Father which art in heaven, hallowed be Thy name. Thy kingdom come. Thy will be done in earth, as it is in

heaven. Give us this day our daily bread. And forgive us our debts, as we forgive our debtors. And lead us not into temptation, but deliver us from evil: For thine is the kingdom, and the power, and the glory, for ever. Amen.
(Benediction)

The Lord bless you and keep you: The Lord make His face to shine upon you, and be gracious to you: The Lord lift up His countenance upon you, and give you peace (Num. 6:24-26, RSV).

or

The grace of the Lord Jesus Christ and the love of God and the fellowship of the Holy Spirit be with you all (2 Cor. 13:14, RSV). Amen.

Adapted from *The Broadman Minister's Manual* by Franklin M. Segler © 1969 Broadman Press. All rights reserved. Used by permission.

LUTHERAN

(Call to Worship)
Pastor: O Lord, open my lips,
Congregation: *and my mouth will declare your praise.*
Pastor: Make haste, O God, to deliver me.
Congregation: *Make haste to help me, O Lord.*

Glory be to the Father and to the Son and to the Holy Spirit; as it was in the beginning, is now, and will be forever. Amen. Praise to you, O Christ. Alleluia.

(The following Psalm may be sung or said.)

The Lord is good and His love endures forever.* His faithfulness continues through all generations. Shout for joy to the Lord,* all the earth. Serve the Lord with gladness;* come before Him with joyful songs. Know that the Lord is God.* It is He who made us, and we are His; we are His people, the sheep of His pasture. Enter His gates with thanksgiving and His courts with praise;* give thanks to Him and praise His name. For the Lord is good and His love endures forever;* His faithfulness continues through all generations. Glory be to the Father and to the Son* and to the Holy Spirit; as it was in the beginning,* is now, and will be forever. Amen. The Lord is good and His love endures forever.* His faithfulness continues through all generations. (Antiphon, Ps. 100:5; Ps. 100)

(Scripture)
Two or more of the following portions of Holy Scripture are
read:
Genesis 2:18-25
Ephesians 5:21-33
John 2:1-11
John 15:12-15
Matthew 19:4-6.
    Ephesians 5:21-33 and Matthew 19:4-6 are always read.

Submit to one another out of reverence for Christ. Wives,
submit to your husbands as to the Lord. For the husband
is the head of the wife as Christ is the head of the
church, his body, of which he is the Savior. Now as the
church submits to Christ, so also wives should submit to
their husbands in everything. Husbands, love your wives,
just as Christ loved the church and gave himself up for
her to make her holy, cleansing her by the washing with
water through the word, and to present her to himself as
a radiant church, without stain or wrinkle or any other
blemish, but holy and blameless. In this same way,
husbands ought to love their wives as their own bodies.
He who loves his wife loves himself. After all, no one ever
hated his own body, but he feeds and cares for it, just as
Christ does the church—for we are members of his body.
"For this reason a man will leave his father and mother
and be united to his wife, and the two will become one
flesh." This is a profound mystery—but I am talking
about Christ and the church. However, each one of you
also must love his wife as he loves himself, and the wife
must respect her husband. (Eph. 5:21-33, NIV)

"Have you not read," he replied, "that at the beginning the
Creator 'made them male and female,' and said, 'For this
reason a man will leave his father and mother and be
united to his wife, and the two will become one flesh'? So
they are no longer two, but one. Therefore what God has
joined together, let man not separate." (Matt. 19:4-6, NIV)

Pastor: O Lord, have mercy on us.
Congregation: *Thanks be to God.*
(Homily)
(Hymn)
(Charge)
    We are gathered here in the sight of God and of His

Church that this man and this woman may be joined together in holy matrimony, which is an honorable estate, which God Himself has instituted and blessed, and by which He gives us a picture of the very communion of Christ and His Bride, the Church. God has both established and sanctified this estate and has promised to bless therein all who love and trust in Him and who seek to give Him their faithful worship and service, for the sake of our Lord Jesus Christ.

God has ordained marriage for the good of man and woman in lifelong companionship according to His good pleasure and that children may be nurtured to the praise of His holy name.

He has further ordained marriage so that the love you have for each other may be hallowed and fulfilled according to His bountiful purposes, both in prosperity and adversity all your days.

Christian marriage consists in your mutual consent, sincerely and freely given, which you now solemnly declare before God, these witnesses, and each other.
(Declaration of Intent)

(G)_____ , will you have this woman to be your wife; to live with her in holy marriage according to the Word of God? Will you love her, comfort her, honor her and keep her, in sickness and in health and, forsaking all others, be husband to her as long as you both shall live?

(G) *I will.*

(B)_____ , will you have this man to be your husband; to live with him in holy marriage according to the Word of God? Will you love him, comfort him, honor him, obey him, and keep him, in sickness and in health and, forsaking all others, be wife to him as long as you both shall live?

(B) *I will.*

(Giving of the Bride)

Who gives this woman to be married to this man?
(Exchange of Vows)

I (G)_____ in the presence of God and these witnesses, take you (B)_____ to be my wife; to have and to hold from this day forward, for better for worse, for richer for poorer, in sickness and in health, to love and to cherish, till death us do part. I pledge you my faithfulness.

I (B)_____ in the presence of God and these witnesses, take you (G)_____ to be my husband; to

have and to hold from this day forward, for better for worse, for richer for poorer, in sickness and in health, to love and to cherish, till death us do part. I pledge you my faithfulness.
(Exchange of Rings)

Grant your blessing, O Lord, to these your servants, that they may be ever mindful of their solemn pledge and, trusting in Your mercy, abound evermore in love through all their days; through Jesus Christ our Lord.
Congregation: *Amen.*

(Said by both.) *Receive this ring as a pledge and token of wedded love and faithfulness.*
(Pronouncement of Marriage)

Join your right hands and kneel.

Forasmuch as _____ and _____ have consented together in holy marriage and have declared the same before God and these witnesses, I therefore pronounce them husband and wife, in the name of the Father and of the Son and of the Holy Spirit. Amen.

What God has joined together, let no one put asunder.
Congregation: *Amen.*

(Hymn)
(Blessing)

The almighty and gracious God abundantly grant you His favor, and sanctify and bless you with the blessing given our first parents in paradise that you may please Him both in body and soul, and live together in holy love until life's end.

The eternal God, the Father of our Lord Jesus Christ, bestow upon you His Holy Spirit, be with you, and richly bless you forever.
Congregation: *Amen.*

(The Lord's Prayer)

In peace, let us pray to the Lord:

Our Father who art in heaven,
  hallowed be Thy name.
Thy kingdom come,
Thy will be done,
  on earth as it is in heaven.
Give us this day our
  daily bread.
And forgive us our trespasses
  as we forgive those
    who trespass against us;
and lead us not into
temptation,
	OR	*Our Father in heaven,*
		  hallowed be Your name.
		Your kingdom come;
		Your will be done,
		  on earth as in heaven.
		Give us today our daily
		  bread.
		And forgive us our sins
		  as we forgive those
		    who sin against us.
		Lead us not into
		temptation,

but deliver us from evil.
For Thine is the kingdom
  and the power and the glory
  forever and ever. Amen

but deliver us from evil.
For the kingdom, the power,
  and the glory are Yours
  now and forever. Amen

Pastor: The Lord be with you.
Congregation: *And with your spirit.*
(Prayer)
Pastor: Let us pray to the Lord.
  Almighty, everlasting God, our heavenly Father, having
  joined this man and woman in holy marriage, grant that
  by Your blessing they may live together according to Your
  Word and promise. Strengthen them in faithfulness and
  love toward each other. Sustain and defend them in all
  trial and temptation, and help them to live in faith toward
  You in the communion of Your holy Church and in loving
  service to each other that they may ever enjoy your
  (heavenly family's) blessing; through Jesus Christ, Your
  Son, our Lord, who lives and reigns with You and the Holy
  Spirit, one God, now and forever.
Congregation: *Amen.*
(Hymn)
(Benediction)
Pastor: The Lord bless you and keep you. The Lord make His
  face shine on you and be gracious to you. The Lord lift up
  His countenance on you and give you peace.
Congregation: *Amen.*

Adapted from the *Lutheran Worship Agenda* © 1983 Concordia Publishing
House. Used by permission.

INTERDENOMINATIONAL

(Presentation of Bride)
Minister: Who gives this woman in marriage?
Father: *I do, on behalf of her mother and me.*
(Call to Worship)
  _____ and _____ welcome you. It is their
desire that you enter into the joy, and beauty, and reverence
of the following moments. Let us worship God.
(Charge)
  Dearly beloved, we are assembled here in the presence of
God, to join this man and this woman in holy marriage;
which is instituted of God, regulated by His commandments,

blessed by our Lord Jesus Christ, and to be held in honor among all men. Let us therefore reverently remember that God has established and sanctified marriage for the welfare and happiness of mankind. Our Savior has declared that a man shall forsake his father and mother and cleave unto his wife. By His apostles, He has instructed those who enter into this relation to cherish a mutual esteem and love; to bear with each other's infirmities and weaknesses; to comfort each other in sickness, trouble, and sorrow; in honor and industry to provide for each other and for their household in temporal things; to pray for and encourage each other in the things which pertain to God; and to live together as heirs of the grace of life.

(Prayer)

(Reading of Scripture)

(Exchange of Vows)

I (G)_____ take thee (B)_____ to my wedded wife, to have and to hold from this day forward, for better for worse, for richer for poorer, in sickness and in health, to love and to cherish, according to God's holy plan, I give you my love.

I (B)_____ take thee (G)_____ to my wedded husband, to have and to hold from this day forward, for better for worse, for richer for poorer, in sickness and in health, to love and to cherish, according to God's holy plan, I give you my love.

(Exchange of Rings)

(G)_____ , what token do you give of your love?

(G) *A ring.*

(G) *With this ring I thee wed, with my body I thee worship, and with all my worldly goods I thee endow; in the name of the Father, and of the Son, and of the Holy Spirit. Amen.*

(Prayer)

Bless, O Lord, these rings to be a symbol of the solemn vows by which this man and this woman have bound themselves to each other in holy matrimony; through Jesus Christ our Lord. Amen.

(Pronouncement of Marriage)

Forasmuch as _____ and _____ have consented together in holy wedlock, and have witnessed the same before God and this congregation, and in so doing have given and pledged their vows to each other, and have declared the same by the giving and receiving of a ring, I pronounce them man and wife together, in the name of the

Father, and of the Son, and of the Holy Spirit. Amen.

Those whom God has joined together let no one put asunder.

(Christ Candle, optional)

Inasmuch as Christ is the Light of the world, and inasmuch as He reigns in your hearts, and it is your desire that your lives burn as one flame for Him, bringing light and life to a dark world—will you now portray your desire.

(Unison Vows of the Christian Home, optional)

Depending upon God for strength and wisdom we pledge ourselves to the establishment of a Christian home. Together we will constantly seek God's will and honor Christ in our marriage.

(Prayer for Couple)

(Presentation)

May I present Mr. and Mrs. _____.

Music

A wedding is a sacred service, as deep and meaningful as a Sunday morning worship service or communion service. Therefore, the music should be scriptural, worshipful, dignified, and well-written. Because of this, some churches may say no to the use of secular love songs and pop, theatrical, and operatic music.

The church organist or minister of music will be able to offer many suggestions of appropriate wedding music. He should be able to direct you to some of the beautiful selections that are not as commonly used. You may still prefer the traditional "Bridal Chorus" from Wagner's *Lohengrin* for the processional and Mendelssohn's "Wedding March" from *Midsummer Night's Dream;* however, there is other music that is equally stirring. At the end of this chapter we've provided lists of some appropriate wedding selections. These lists are by no means exhaustive, but they will at least provide a starting point for you as you search for specific music for your wedding.

SELECTING THE MUSIC

Record and tape libraries are available in many localities. These facilities will either let you check out records or will pro-vide a room in which you can listen to them. Take the time to listen to classical music and to make selections both you and your groom appreciate. Consult the librarian if you have any questions. Also, some music stores have listings of sacred and secular wedding music to help you.

Consider music for the different parts of the ceremony.

- Organ preludes can be used as introductions to the more important music that is to come. The organist should start about a half hour before the wedding. He should play softly in the background while the guests are being seated and the candles are being lit.
- In some circles it is the norm for a small musical ensemble to play before the wedding begins. They should end with a piece that is on the soft side as the mothers are being seated.
- A solo would be appropriate right before the processional. It can be used to turn the thoughts of the guests to reflect on the wedding. This may be a selection of endearment or a hymn of praise.
- The processional announces the wedding party as they enter the sanctuary. A special selection or an increase in volume occurs as the bride appears.

WEDDING MUSIC CHECKLIST

Fees

Ceremony Date _____ Time _____ $ _____

Minister of music _____ Phone _____

Organist _____ Phone _____ _____

Church policy:

Appointment: Date _____ Time _____

Suggested selections:

   Prelude

   Processional

   Solos

   Hymns

   Recessional

   Postlude

   Special music for mothers

Out-of-church organist practice time_____

Other musicians:

   Appointment date _____ Time _____ _____

WEDDING MUSIC CHECKLIST (cont.)

Suggested selections:

Reception music:

Musician: _____

    Appointment date _____ Time _____   _____

Suggested selections:

Special fanfare _____   _____

Gifts _____   _____

Rehearsal dinner _____   _____

                                        Total $ _____

- As the processional ends, a hymn may be sung with the guests participating in an attitude of worship. However, a moment of quietness before the minister begins the wedding ceremony would also be appropriate.
- A solo after the vows or while kneeling gives time for continued reflection. Chimes may be used.
- After the pronouncement and introduction, a triumphant selection is in order for the recessional.
- Lively music may be played as the guests depart.

Consider these guidelines:

- You may be thinking of singing for your own wedding. Some ministers prefer that the bride and groom not do this. Singing at your own wedding may increase your anxiety; you may become so nervous that you muff your part. Also, some people interpret this as an inappropriate display of talent. A solo may, however, be recorded ahead of time and then played during the ceremony (with the couple facing the altar).

- Certain selections may be used as "cues," such as the time when the processional is about to begin.
- A particular selection could be played as the mothers are seated.
- If there is no instrumental music available, recorded music can be used. It is best to avoid music with a dominant beat or a sensual sound. If you are not going to have live music, consider using tapes instead of records.

SELECTING THE MUSICIANS

Generally a bride and groom will be interested in procuring the services of both instrumentalists and vocalists. In either case, the fee for musicians is usually taken up with each individual. Even if you know any of the musicians personally, a remuneration is still expected. Time and traveling expenses should also be covered. Feel free to include them at the rehearsal dinner, too.

You are responsible for providing any sheet music. Get it to the performers as early as possible, so they will have plenty of time to rehearse.

If you prefer not to have a vocalist, or if a good one is not available, instrumental pieces are just as nice. There are many combinations of instruments that can be used: piano and organ, flute and oboe, violin and flute, organ and harp or violin, or violin and cello, just to name a few. A single trumpet, brass quartet, woodwind ensemble, or a guitar are also good choices. More elaborate weddings may even have a choir, madrigal singers, or a bell choir. Remember, though, that special musical arrangements will require extra work and perhaps an extra rehearsal.

The organ, of course, is the traditional instrument for wedding music; but you may decide to use a piano in its place. This is nice in a church where there is a particularly beautiful piano and an exceptional pianist. A harp is another alternative to the organ.

Before you hire anyone, check with the church to see if it requires you to use its own musicians. If that is not the case, and you don't know anyone musically inclined, you may be tempted to go to the local music school, high school, or college for musicians. But a word of caution: Amateurs may be more economical, but professionals give the best results. If at all possible, don't leave yourself open for surprises! Instead, consult the minister of music or organist for recommendations of local talented musicians.

REHEARSAL GUIDELINES

Use the Musician's Guidelines form in this chapter to make a list of the musical selections in the order they are to be sung or played, and give a copy of this to each musician.

The musicians must be present at the wedding rehearsal and play the beginning and ending of each accompaniment so that the participants are aware of which pieces are being played and where they fit into the wedding ceremony. If there are several musicians, ask them to have a full rehearsal before the wedding rehearsal.

Check with the church for folders and music stands for the musicians. Arrange for the musicians' seating area and the best location for any soloists and musicians who need to stand. Also find out

MUSICIAN'S GUIDELINES

Wedding of _____ Date _____ Arrive at _____
Organist _____ Phone _____

TIME   **SELECTIONS**   **MUSICIAN**
                  Preludes

    Solo

    Solo

    Processional

    Ceremony music

    Recessional

    Postlude

Soloists:
Name _____ Phone _____
Name _____ Phone _____
Instrumentalists or choir members:
Name _____ Phone _____
Name _____ Phone _____
Name _____ Phone _____
Name _____ Phone _____

Special rehearsal date _____ Time _____
Wedding rehearsal date _____ Time _____
What to wear for wedding: _____

about placement of any sound equipment for them. Any tuning of the piano or organ should be done a day or two in advance.

RECEPTION MUSIC

A background of music will provide a relaxed and pleasant atmosphere for greeting your guests. It should be light in tone in order to be conducive to conversation. Classical music is not recommended for this since it can get loud and intense in places.

A single piano, violin, guitar, harp, piano and strings, or a string trio will keep the receiving or buffet line moving along. The musicians should play lively, familiar tunes. Consider using tapes which you can rent or prepare ahead of time. If continuous music is desired, a happy combination of "live" music and taped music may be considered. Otherwise, arrange for more than one musician to play.

Some families have a program at a seated reception, including musical selections of a lighter nature by friends or family. A reception card may request that the guests bring their talent to be presented as a gift to the bridal couple. A piano would then need to be provided.

Here are some guidelines for music at the reception:

- Check to see that the piano is tuned.
- Arrange for a place to seat the musicians. Instrumentalists will also need a place to store their instrument cases.
- Give the musicians a list of favorite songs.
- Suggest what they should wear.
- Give them sheet music ahead of time to practice.
- Pay them individually with checks before they leave.

- If you like, fanfares could be played when you and your groom arrive at the reception, before the cutting of the cake, and before the throwing of the bouquet.

MUSICAL SELECTIONS

Preludes:

Bach—Abide with Us, Lord Jesus Christ
　　　Adagio
　　　Arioso
　　　God's Time Is Best
　　　Jesu, Joy of Man's Desiring
　　　Sheep May Safely Graze
　　　Siciliano
　　　Sleepers Awake
Bonnet—Romance Sans Paroles
Brahms—Behold, a Rose is Blooming
　　　My Jesus Calls to Me
Dupre—Preludes on Antiphone
Gillette—Chant d'Amour
Handel—Adagio in E from Violin Sonata
　　　Air from Water Music Suite
　　　Aria in F major
James—Meditation of Sainte Clotilde
Kreckel—Lo, How a Rose Appeareth
Mendelssohn—Consolation
　　　　On Wings of Song
Pachelbel—Canon
Peeters—Now Thank We All Our God
Purcell—Bell Symphony
　　　Voluntary in C major
Vivaldi—Spring from the Four Seasons

Processionals:

Bach—Adagio from Toccata in C major
　　　Jesu, Joy of Man's Desiring
　　　Sinfonia from Wedding Cantata
Beethoven—Ode to Joy (Hymn of Joy)
　　　　(Theme from Ninth Symphony)
Bloch—Four Wedding Marches

Brahms—St. Anthony's Chorale
    Variations on a
    Theme by Haydn
Campra—Rigaudon
Domini—When Morning Gilds the Sky
Franck—Fantasie in C
Handel—Air from Water Music Suite
    Allegro Maestoso from Water
    Music Suite
    Aria in F major
    Thanks Be to Thee
Jongen—Rondeau from Sinfonies de
    Fanfare
Purcell—Trumpet Tune in D major
    Trumpet Voluntary in D major
    (both sometimes attributed to
    Jeremiah Clark)
    Trumpet Voluntaire
    Praise, My Soul, the King of
    Heaven (Westminster Abbey)
Rheinberger—Cantilena
Telemann—Concerto in A minor
Wachs—Pas des Bouquetieres (March of
    the Flower Girls)
Wagner—Bridal Chorus from Lohengrin
Such hymns as: Praise to the Lord, the
    Almighty

Vocal Solos:
Bach—Be Thou But Near
    Jesu, Joy of Man's Desiring
Barnby—O Perfect Love
Beethoven—Joyful, Joyful, We Adore
    Thee
Burleigh—O Perfect Love
Clokey— O Perfect Love
Cook—Follow You
Crouch—My Tribute
Dungan—Eternal Life (prayer of
    St. Francis of Assisi)
Dunlap—The Wedding Prayer
Dvorak—I Will Sing New Songs
    of Gladness
    (from Biblical Songs)

Franck—Panis Angelicus (O Lord Most
    Holy)
Gladden—O Master, Let Them Walk with
    Thee
Grieg—Ich Liebe Dich (So Love I Thee)
d'Hardelot—Because
Hinsworth—The King of Love My
    Shepherd Is
Honeytree—Ruth
Hopson—The Gift of Love
Hummel—Alleluia
Johnson—Make Us One
    Violin Obligato
Keble-Dykes—The Voice That Breathed
    O'er Eden
Malan—Take Our Lives
Malotte—The Lord's Prayer
Mendelssohn—A Wedding Prayer
    A. Gibbs Tune
    Consolation
Morrison (arr.)—Alleluia
Mozart—Alleluia
Peterson—Of Love I Sing
Robb—Because He First Loved Me
Schütz—Wedding Prayer
    Wedding Song (Song of Ruth)
Singer—Song of Ruth
Stewart—Our Heart's Prayer
Thiman—Thou Wilt Keep Him in
    Perfect Peace
Williams—A Wedding Prayer
Wise—Take Our Bread

Wedding Prayer Hymns:
Be Thou My Vision (Tune: Slane)
Children of the Heavenly Father
He Leadeth Me
If Thou but Suffer God to Guide Thee
The King of Love My Shepherd Is
Like a Lamb Who Needs the Shepherd
Like a River Glorious
Make Us Willing
May the Mind of Christ My Saviour
O Perfect Love

The Lord's My Shepherd (Tunes: Crimond, also Brother James' Air)

Instrumental Solos:
Bradbury—Saviour, Like a Shepherd Lead Us
Corelli—Adagio from Sonata (Opus 5 No. 1)
Glazounow—Meditation (violin)
Herbert—O Love That Wilt Not Let Me Go
Massenet—Meditation from Thais
Smith—O Master, Let Me Walk with Thee

Choral Ensembles:
Atkinson—Spirit of God
Schubert—Thou Lovely One (arr.)

Hymns for Congregational Participation:
Children of the Heavenly Father
How Great Thou Art
Like a River Glorious
We Rest in Thee
When We Walk with the Lord (Trust and Obey)
The Lord Bless You and Keep You

Recessionals:
Beethoven—Ode to Joy from Symphony #9
Couperin—Chaconne
Handel—Allegro Maestoso from Water Music Suite
Postlude in G major
Processional in G major
Karg-Elert—Now Thank We All Our God
Marcello—Psalm XIX
Mendelssohn—Wedding March from Mid-summer Night's Dream
Purcell—Bell Symphony
Trumpet Voluntary in D major
Trumpet Tune in D major
Soler—The Emperor's Fanfare
Stolzel—Sonata in D major

Wesley—Choral Song
Widor—Allegro vivace from Symphony #5
Toccata from Symphony #5
Young—Hymn to Joy
Such hymns as: Joyful, Joyful We Adore Thee
Love Divine, All Loves Excelling
Now Thank We All Our God

Here are some suggestions of composers of organ music suitable for preludes and postludes:

Baroque	Bach
	Buxtehude
	Corelli
	Couperin
	Froberger
	Handel
	Mouret
	Pachelbel
	Purcell
	Soler
Classic	Mozart
	Schubert
Romantic	Brahms
	Franck
	Karg-Elert
	Mendelssohn
20th Century	Langlais
	Manz
	Peeters
	Vaughan Williams
	Walcha
	Willan

Processionals, recessionals, and service music can be found in such outstanding collections as:

● Wedding Music, Vols. I & II—ed. by Bunjes (Concordia)

- Wedding Music for the Church Organist and Soloist—ed. by Lovelace (Abingdon)
- Wedding Music, Vols. I & II—ed. by Johnson (Augsburg)
- Ceremonial Music for Organ, Vols. I & II—ed. by Christopher Dearnley (Oxford)
- Wedding Music for the Organ—ed. by Homer Whitford (Flammer)
- Wedding Blessings—ed. by Bunjes (Concordia) (vocal solos with organ and instrumental accompaniments)

Programs

It is not a necessity, but the printed wedding program is a practical addition to any wedding ceremony. Its purpose is to help the guests follow the order of service and identify the people involved. You may express your sincere thanks to your guests through the program as well.

The program is usually made up just before the wedding in order to include any last-minute changes. However, the covers may be purchased ahead of time to match the color and theme of the invitations. A satin ribbon can be tied along the fold for an elegant touch.

You may type the program yourself or have a calligrapher do it in beautiful lettering. For best results, though, you may want to have a print shop specially typeset it. Whichever way you choose, remember that what you bring in to the print shop to have run off is what you will get.

Be sure that each page is exactly the way you want it, with all errors neatly corrected. Leave at least a half-inch margin at the top, bottom, and sides of each page. The program can be printed on one or two sides, whichever you prefer. Allow a week to have it finished. Note: Quick-print places do a satisfactory job, especially if the program has already been typeset.

TITLE SUGGESTIONS FOR CEREMONY PARTS

The Wedding Ceremony

The Marriage Uniting in Christ . . .

Welcome to the Marriage Ceremony of . . .

The Celebration of the Marriage in Christ of . . .

A Service of Holy Matrimony Uniting . . .

A Celebration of the Covenant of Marriage of . . .

Rings

The Giving of the Rings

The Ring Ceremony

Presenting of the Rings

Giving and Receiving of Rings

Ring Service

Exchange of Vows and Rings

Candlelighting

Lighting of the Candles

The Candlelighting Ceremony

Uniting of the Candles

Lighting of the Christ Candle

Message

The Mystery of Marriage
Pastoral Counsel to Couple
God's Plan for Marriage
Reflections on Christian Marriage
Minister's Charge
Words of Advice and Counsel
Meditation
Charge to the Bride and Groom
Address to the Couple
The Significance of Marriage
Words of Encouragement:
  to the Couple
  to the Congregation
Challenge

PERSONAL TOUCHES

A Note of Thanks

If you and your groom want a special message printed on the program, use the following examples to create your own. Write a few simple words of thanksgiving and praise that express your feelings.

We thank you for coming to be with us on this very special day of our lives. During the ceremony, vows will be spoken, but far more important than these are the love, trust, and commitment which we feel toward each other and Christ our Lord.

To our parents:
Thank you for the patience, care, and understanding that have led to this joy-

ful day. Praise be to God from whom all blessings flow.

We wish to express our joy and appreciation on this very special day in our lives to each of you who came to be with us and share in our happiness.

Believing that God has led us together, and pledging to honor God's will above all else, it is our prayer that God will lead us as we build a Christian home, and use us to further His glory. It is also our prayer that this day of commitment for us will be a day of renewed commitment for each of you.

Thank you for sharing this joyous celebration with us!

Appropriate Scripture and Poetry

The following are some suitable scriptural passages that can be used on the wedding program:

"Delight thyself also in the Lord; and he shall give thee the desires of thine heart." (Psalm 37:4)

"Set me as a seal upon your heart,
  as a seal upon your arm;
for love is strong as death. . . .
Many waters cannot quench love,
  neither can floods drown it."
(Song of Solomon 8:6, 7, RSV)

"O magnify the Lord with me, and let

us exalt his name together." (Psalm 34:3)

"We love him, because he first loved us." (1 John 4:19)

"Beloved, let us love one another; for love is of God, and he who loves is born of God and knows God." (1 John 4:7, RSV)

"Trust in the Lord with all thine heart; and lean not unto thine own understanding. In all thy ways acknowledge him, and he shall direct thy paths." (Proverbs 3:5, 6)

"For because of our faith, he has brought us into this place of highest privilege where we now stand, and we confidently and joyfully look forward to actually becoming all that God has had in mind for us to be." (Romans 5:2, TLB)

"Wither thou goest, I will go; and where thou lodgest, I will lodge: thy people shall be my people, and thy God my God." (Ruth 1:16)

"Unless the Lord builds the house, those who build it labor in vain." (Psalm 127:1, RSV)

"Love is patient, love is kind. It does not envy, it does not boast, it is not proud.

It always protects, always trusts, always hopes, always perseveres." (1 Corinthians 13:4, 7, NIV)

"The man who finds a wife finds a good thing; she is a blessing to him from the Lord." (Proverbs 18:22, TLB)

"Husbands, in the same way be considerate as you live with your wives, and treat them with respect as the weaker partner and as heirs with you of the gracious gift of life, so that nothing will hinder your prayers." (1 Peter 3:7, NIV)

"His love is perfected in us." (1 John 4:12, RSV)

"Walk in love, as Christ also hath loved us." (Ephesians 5:2)

"I will be their God. And I will give them one heart. . . ." (Jeremiah 32:38, 39, TLB)

If you have room for more than one verse (perhaps on the back of the program), some passages you may want to consider are Ephesians 5:25-33; Ephesians 5:21-24, 33; 1 Peter 3:1-4; and Proverbs 31:10-30.

Often words to a favorite or especially appropriate hymn are printed on the program. Another way to add your own personal touch is to include a famous poem on love, or, if you are so inclined, to write one of your own.

RECEPTION PROGRAMS

An alternative to the wedding program is the reception program. A simple folded sheet with a picture of you and the groom might be copied along with the menu and the names of those in the wedding party. Information about each person could be given—where he is from, and where you and/or the groom met the person. Other things could be added, such as your thanks to the guests, a prayer for your lives, and your plans for the future. You might even include a few fun songs for all of the guests to sing.

PROGRAM (WEDDING OR RECEPTION)

Stationer or printer _____ Phone _____

Cover _____

Description _____ Number to be ordered _____

Cost _____

FORM FOR THE PROGRAM

Checklists & Worksheets

There are many plans that need to be kept in order in the months preceding a wedding. How smoothly your wedding runs is dependent on a good recording system.

Begin with a card file of 3″ x 5″ cards to keep your guest list in order. After gathering everyone's guest lists, record each complete name, address, zip code, and phone number on a card, and place the cards in alphabetical order. Mark on each card whether an invitation has been sent, a gift received, and a thank-you note sent. If there are some people to whom you are only sending announcements keep their cards separate. Also, keep a card for each professional whose services you are using.

There are many lists in this chapter provided for your convenience. Feel free to write on them as you need to.

Two lists in particular are of utmost importance. The first is the guest list. After you have recorded the information on your 3″ x 5″ cards, transfer this to the list provided. This way you will have fast and easy access to the guest information as well as a permanent file for the future (for Christmas cards, etc.). Give the groom's mother a copy of this list for her information.

Another important list is the Gift Record. A place is provided here to record gifts as you receive them. Number each gift on the list and place a corresponding number sticker on the gift itself. Always write a description and the date received. Use this list (which lists the gifts) along with the card file (which lists the addresses) when writing thank-yous.

Another way to keep yourself organized is to use an engagement calendar. One is provided in this chapter. Begin by checking off those things that have already been decided on, and work from there. Add other things you will need to do that are specific to your wedding. If you have one master list of all the errands you need to run, people you need to contact, etc., you will always feel you are in control (and in fact, you will be!).

SAMPLE FILE CARD

Name _____
Address _____
_____
Phone _____

Invitation _____
Announcement _____
Gift received _____
Thank-you sent _____

MASTER GUEST LIST

(Last names in alphabetical order. Cross off regrets.)

NAME	NUMBER ATTENDING RECEPTION

MASTER GUEST LIST (cont.)

NAME	NUMBER ATTENDING RECEPTION

GIFT RECORD				
NO.	GIFT	DATE	GIVEN BY	DESCRIPTION

NO.	GIFT	DATE	GIVEN BY	DESCRIPTION
GIFT RECORD (cont.)				

Bride's Engagement Calendar

As soon as you are engaged, announce it at a party, in the newspaper, and in visits to friends.

A year to six months before the wedding:

____ Make an appointment with the minister and talk over the date and time for the ceremony.

____ Think through your priorities—budget, formality, reception site, and number of guests. (See chapter 3.)

____ You will want to shop around—get prices and samples. Check out florists, photographers, bakeries, gowns, caterers, rings, invitations, and travel agencies for honeymoon arrangements.

____ Reserve the reception site and/or caterer.

____ Select a photographer and make arrangements with him for the wedding day.

____ It will take time to select things for the gift registry. Go back more than once. Take your time looking around to be sure you register for what would best suit your needs.

____ Write your fiancé's parents about the plans.

____ Contact the local newspapers about your engagement and upcoming wedding.

Six months—no later than four months: (Complete above first.)

____ Decide on your attendants. Choose their dresses and get them set up for fittings.

____ Make a list of attendants' (including ushers') names, addresses, and phone numbers and distribute to friends and relatives to be sure that they're included in prewedding activities.

____ Go with your mother to look at dresses for her.

____ Choose your wedding gown, veil, and accessories.

____ Reserve a florist.

____ Work on the guest list; set a deadline for everyone's to be finished. Enter the list in your card file along with the attendants, services, stores.

____ Start premarital counseling classes.

____ Plan the wording for the wedding invitations.

Three months:

____ Order the invitations and start addressing them as soon as you receive them.

____ Order the men's attire with your fiancé and finalize your mother's selection for her dress. Remind her to let the groom's mother know the style and color.

____ Make medical (physical, dental, and eye) appointments for six weeks before the wedding.

____ Start shopping for housing if you need it and for furniture if you plan to purchase some pieces. Take your time.

____ Shop for your trousseau, for thank-you gifts, and check out the garage sales for nice little household items.

____ This is the time for parties and showers. Be thinking of who should be invited in case you're asked.

____ Plan the music for the wedding and reception.

____ Plan the bridesmaid's party.

____ Look into any business details. Check with a lawyer on legal matters, if necessary.

___ Fill in your attendants on all of the latest plans.

___ If an at-home wedding, arrange for services needed such as a gardener or extra household help.

Two months:

___ Plan the rehearsal with the wedding coordinator and the ceremony with the minister and your fiancé.

___ Plan the reception down to the last detail.

___ Assist in planning the rehearsal dinner, if needed.

___ Order the cake.

___ Purchase the wedding rings.

___ Make reservations at hotels for accommodations for out-of-town guests.

___ Begin the countdown with your groom, reading the Psalms. Start with the sixtieth and read one each day in descending order to Psalm 1 for your wedding day.

During one month before:

___ Have your teeth cleaned.

___ Have your hair cut.

___ Purchase any grooming accessories you may need.

___ Mail the invitations.

___ Keep up the master list of acceptances.

___ Enter gift descriptions in gift record.

___ Write thank-you notes. Enter in card file.

___ Prepare programs for wedding and/or reception.

___ Prepare seating charts/place cards for rehearsal dinner and reception.

___ Write up form for newspaper wedding announcement (to be sent with a picture after the wedding).

___ Address announcements.

___ Make a time agenda for the wedding day.

___ Buy and wrap attendants' gifts (gift for the groom).

___ Plan table for gift display at home.

___ Go with groom for marriage license.

___ Have bridal portrait taken.

One week:

___ Have final fitting of wedding gown.

___ Give caterer definite number of reception guests.

___ Send out reminders for rehearsal.

___ Pack for wedding trip and prepare going-away handbag.

___ Get things together to bring to rehearsal.

___ Double-check all plans. Meet with the church wedding coordinator for a walk through on the rehearsal morning, if possible.

Wedding day:

___ Enjoy the day!

GROOM'S CHECKLIST

A year to six months:

___ Enjoy the glow of your bride as she tells the world of your engagement.

___ Make arrangements to meet with the minister to set a date and time for the wedding.

___ Assist your fiancée in deciding on the gift registry.

___ Make medical (physical, dental, and eye) appointments for six weeks before wedding. Check to see if you will need inoculations if you're going out of the country for your honeymoon.

Six months to four months:

____ Start working on your guest list with your parents.

____ Shop for wedding rings.

____ Select your best man, groomsmen and/or ushers. (Generally one usher for every fifty guests is a good rule.)

____ Begin planning the honeymoon.

Three months:

____ Order wedding attire.

____ Consult parents on arrangements for rehearsal dinner.

____ Check with florist on order of flowers for bride, mother, etc.

____ Purchase personal gift for bride. (Clothing would not be suitable in this case.)

____ Shop with fiancée for future housing and furniture.

Two months:

____ Work on ceremony plans with bride and minister.

____ Shop for clothing needs.

____ Arrange for transportation/accommodations for wedding party and out-of-town guests.

____ Purchase wedding rings.

____ Have honeymoon arrangements finalized, if at all possible.

____ Begin the countdown with your bride, reading the Psalms, starting with the sixtieth and reading one each day in descending order to Psalm 1 for your wedding day.

One month:

____ Have duplicate car keys made; car tuned up.

GOING FOR THE WEDDING LICENSE

Date _____ Time _____

County Clerk's Office   Phone _____   Fee _____

_____   Waiting period _____

_____

_____

Requirements: *Bride*   *Groom*

Physician's certificate
   Blood test

Identification:
   Birth certificate (if under age)
   Citizenship papers
   Driver's license
   Other

License is valid _____ days.

(The bride and groom should contact the County Clerk's office for information regarding the wedding license. Regulations differ from state to state.)

_____ Go with fiancée for marriage license.

_____ Keep medical appointments; get financial affairs in order.

_____ Make sure all medical, religious, and legal documents are in order. Call your insurance agent for advice on changing beneficiaries. You may need to visit a lawyer.

_____ Have hair trimmed.

One week:

_____ Take your best man and ushers to a sports event and stop for an informal snack afterward.

_____ Pack; wrap gifts; check wedding attire; have honorarium in envelope for best man to give to pastor after the ceremony.

_____ At rehearsal dinner, give gifts to men, gift to bride-to-be.

_____ Partially fill in license.

Wedding day:

_____ Be on time for the wedding! (Check with the bride on the time schedule.)

_____ After the reception, spend a few moments alone with your parents for good-byes.

_____ The day after the wedding, send a telegram or phone both sets of parents. You will have much to thank them for. Express to them what a memorable event your wedding day was.

The following appointments calendar is for you to use to keep all wedding-related appointments in order. (Make copies for more than one month.) Be sure you schedule time for each of the following:

Medical:
    Gynecologist
    Dental
    Eye
Professionals:
    Minister
    Florist
    Photographer
    Lawyer
    Organist
    Other
Bakery
Bridal shop
Caterer
Musicians
Hairdresser
Seamstress
Wedding Hostess/Coordinator
Car tune up
Gift registry consultant

SCHEDULE OF APPOINTMENTS

SUNDAY				SUNDAY			
MONDAY				MONDAY			
TUESDAY				TUESDAY			
WEDNESDAY				WEDNESDAY			
THURSDAY				THURSDAY			
FRIDAY				FRIDAY			
SATURDAY				SATURDAY			

SUNDAY				SUNDAY			
MONDAY				MONDAY			
TUESDAY				TUESDAY			
WEDNESDAY				WEDNESDAY			
THURSDAY				THURSDAY			
FRIDAY				FRIDAY			
SATURDAY				SATURDAY			

ACCOMMODATIONS				
GUEST	HOST OR HOTEL	ARRIVE	LEAVE	COST
			Total	$ _____

PLANNING THE REHEARSAL DINNER

Make reservation:

Date _____ Time _____

Location _____ Number of guests _____

GUESTS:	Address	Phone

MENU	COST

DECORATIONS (flowers, candles)	

Subtotal $ _____

Gratuities $ _____

Total $ _____

PROGRAM: M.C. _____

CUSTODIAN'S WORKSHEET

Give to church custodian a week before the wedding.

Wedding of _____ and _____

Rehearsal date _____ Time _____

Sanctuary

    Set up:

        Candelabra _____

        Kneeling bench _____

        Other _____

    Articles to remove:

    Double-check:

Diagram of platform set-up.

Other instructions:

Wedding date _____ Time _____

Church should be open by _____

Wedding party arrives at _____

    Set up:

        Rooms for dressing _____

Double-check sanctuary set-up above.

Please clean floor after florist leaves.

Church reception area

Cleaned and set up by _____

Caterer _____

Time of arrival _____

Number of guests expected _____

    Set up:

        Tables _____

        Chairs _____

Kitchen:

Diagram of reception set-up.

Florist will pick up _____ at _____

Duties

THE MAID OF HONOR

Every bride has an honor attendant, known as the maid of honor (or matron of honor if she is married). A maid of honor who is conscientious about her traditional duties can be a great help to the bride. She should pay for her own attire, which is chosen by the bride. The maid of honor and the best man are the official witnesses to the ceremony, and they sign the marriage certificate as such. The maid of honor gives special attention to the bride's needs, acting as her lady-in-waiting. She helps her dress, and during the wedding adjusts her veil and train, and may smooth the blusher veil back if the bride wears one. She holds the bride's bouquet during the ceremony and keeps the groom's ring on one of her fingers until the rings are exchanged.

Before the wedding, the maid of honor should practice draping the train of the bride's dress in the appropriate way. She should also rehearse fixing the bustle of the dress for the receiving line. Sandpaper can be rubbed on the bottom of the bride's shoes to prevent her from slipping on carpeting.

In the receiving line, the maid of honor stands next to the groom, and sits next to him at a sit-down dinner reception. She helps the bride change after the wedding and sees to it that the best man gets the luggage. She tells the bride's parents when the bride and groom are about to leave. She is expected to pick up after the bride leaves and assist the bride's mother in any way she can.

Most important, though, she listens. The bride will need a friend who will give encouragement and support through all of the planning.

THE BRIDESMAIDS

The bridesmaids may be sisters of the bride or good friends. (Consider choosing one of the groom's sisters to join in the wedding party.) They are called "bridesmaids" regardless of their marital status.

In some countries it is the custom to have a number of very young girls as bridesmaids. The wedding of Prince Charles and Princess Diana of England was an example of that. In the United States, however, the bride's close friends and sisters who are closer to her own age are usually invited to participate.

The bridesmaids are expected to pay for their own dresses and accessories, which the bride picks out. They may stand in the receiving line if the bride so desires. At the reception, the bridesmaids are expected to be attentive to the guests. They pay for their own transportation to the wedding.

THE JUNIOR BRIDESMAIDS

Bride's attendants under the age of sixteen are considered junior bridesmaids. Young girls are usually enthralled with the idea of being in a wedding. You may prefer to use these girls as candlelighters, or, you may give them the duty of passing out little packets of rice, or little boxes of the groom's cake (if you decide to have one at your reception).

Junior bridesmaids are usually not included in the receiving line.

It is expected that all the bridesmaids will pay for their own wedding attire, but your parents may choose to pay, or arrange to have the dresses made to order. The junior bridesmaids' dresses should be modified versions of the bridesmaids' dresses.

THE FLOWER GIRL

The flower girl is a very young girl with a basket of flowers or rose petals who walks in front of the bride. It usually happens that she is a bit nervous or emotional; this can cause one or two tense moments right before she walks down the aisle. She may need some gentle reassurance. If she is under four years old, her mother or sister should attend her, and someone should be responsible for her after she reaches the front. If she's quite young, it's usually best to have her join her family in their pew at the front. She does not have to take part in the reces-

sional. Her dress may be long or short, and should blend in with the color scheme.

THE BEST MAN

The best man can be of great help to the groom if he is aware of his responsibilities. He is usually a very close friend or brother, and is the official male witness of the wedding who signs the marriage certificate. He will carry the wedding ring for the bride to the ceremony and see that the groom is properly attired and on time for the ceremony. It is important to pick someone who can be trusted with your car keys and any tickets needed for the honeymoon. He will also be the one to make sure the minister's fee is sealed in an envelope and ready to be handed to the minister. The best man may give the announcements at the reception and offer a short speech of congratulations to the bride and groom.

If no one else is in charge, he will see to directing the ushers or appoint a head usher, and take charge of gathering the men's attire after the wedding. He should see that the wedding license is filled in and signed and that the bridal party leaves in the right cars. He checks on the honeymoon details such as the car, the reservations, luggage, and any other transportation; he summons the groom's parents to say good-bye, and has the groom's car safe and ready for the getaway.

He is usually one of the last ones to collapse. As you can see, he is a very busy man!

THE USHERS

The ushers are an important part of the wedding party. They are close friends or relatives of the groom (or yourself). They usher the guests, as well as participate in the wedding as needed (they may also be the groomsmen). Ushers pay for the rental of their clothing which usually includes gloves (if worn), tie, and jewelry. Shoes may be rented as well to match the formality of the outfit.

The ushers should be well-informed of their duties since they will have many responsibilities. There should be a specific time set aside during the rehearsal to give them their instructions. They will also need time to practice any special moves, such as the candlelighting.

If a head usher is selected, he can be responsible for assigning the various ushers to the other posts. If he is familiar with the family and relatives, he can be given the honor of ushering them to their reserved sections. He could also draw the aisle runner back.

The specific duties of the ushers are to:

1. Be in the narthex forty-five minutes before the wedding. They should be familiar with the locations of various entrances, exits, and restrooms in the church.

2. Greet the early guests and make pleasant conversation with them if needed.

3. Usher the guests. As more people arrive and the organ begins to play, the ushers should line up on the left side of the center aisle door (or wherever the ushering is to be done from). They will then be in the correct position to offer the lady their right arm.

Ask the guests if they are friends or relatives of the bride, or friends or relatives of the groom. Friends and relatives of the bride are seated to the left of the center aisle; friends and relatives of the groom to the right. The bride and groom may prefer the usher not ask anything more than whether the guest is a friend or relative; then the guests may be seated evenly on both sides. Close relatives are usually seated in the reserved pews behind the parents. If you have sent out pew cards (see chapter 11) with your invitations, the guests should show them to the ushers, and then be seated in the designated pews.

The usher should offer his right arm and walk the lady to her seat. The husband or escort will follow. If a woman mistakenly takes the usher's left arm, he should proceed without notice.

4. Seat the guests. Turn to stand in front of the pew to face the lady as she enters the pew. Wait until she is seated before offering her a program. On the left, the lady should be allowed to walk across in front of the usher. At the same time, he should make a counter-clockwise move to stand in front of the pew to face her as she enters. Wait until she is seated, and then offer her a program. Proceed to the back to continue ushering.

Guests should be seated from front to back in the sanctuary. When the center aisle is full, the ushering should be continued at the side aisles.

Variations: When ushering at the right aisle, the left arm may be offered. In the case where several ladies are together, the more elderly should be ushered first. The others may follow or wait to be ushered in separately. The usher should walk beside a single man to his seat. If the man is infirm or handicapped, the usher may offer his arm if needed.

5. Escort special guests. Often certain ushers are assigned to escort special relatives or friends to their seats.

6. Light the candles at the designated time. Check the wicks in the torches for adjustments. Watch as candles are lighted

to guard against wicks going out. If there are two candlelighters, they should watch each other and light the candles simultaneously. Start with the lowest or first candle and go to the highest or last. The ushers should be informed which candles to light in the Christ candelabra (the two outside ones or none at all).

7. Lay the aisle runner. Two ushers are usually needed for this. They should grasp the outside corners of the runner, pull firmly, and not jerk. They should face forward while going up the aisle, glancing over their shoulders occasionally to check that the runner is straight. Or, if the runner has a rope or handle, it may require only one usher.

8. Seat the parents. The mother of the groom is ushered to the second pew on the right, followed by the father of the groom, unless otherwise instructed. Then the mother of the bride is ushered into the second pew on the left. (The first pews are kept empty.) If there is no center aisle, both sets of parents are seated in the center section, the middle of the center section being the dividing line. The right aisle is usually used for the processional, and the left for the recessional.

9. Ask late guests to slip into seats off the side aisles. No ushering should be done after the mother of the bride is seated. Ushers who are to participate in the wedding as groomsmen will leave at a pre-arranged time to join the groom and best man.

10. Usher the mothers out after the recessional in any of the following ways:

- Four ushers come forward to the top of the aisle and turn around clockwise. Two remain standing there while focusing forward. One of the others nods to the bride's parents. They rise and the usher offers his arm to the mother. She is escorted out as the father follows. Then the other usher nods to the groom's parents and escorts them out in the same manner. (The mother may take the usher's left arm in this case.) The other two ushers remain at the top of the aisle while the first two ushers come back and usher out any elderly guests or special relatives sitting in the front pews. (The first two ushers then allow the other guests to exit row by row.)
- The above procedure can be done with two ushers, if you prefer.
- Another way is for the ushers to remain standing in place while the bride's parents walk arm in arm up the aisle together. After the groom's parents have done the same, the ushers may proceed to let the guests exit.

11. Extinguish the candles after the grandparents are ushered out, if the bride so chooses. This gives the family a few moments to greet each other, and completes the candlelighting ritual.

12. Dismiss the guests by a nod of the head, one row at a time, beginning at the front of the church on the bride's side and alternating rows. Otherwise, the guests may be allowed to exit on their own, without direction.

13. Other miscellaneous duties are

- Put street barricades in place, if necessary.
- Open the church doors as the bride and groom exit.
- Direct guests to the reception.
- Pass out maps.
- Check the dressing rooms for forgotten items.

THE RING BEARER

The ring bearer is a small boy who carries a pillow on which plastic rings are sewn, or on which the real rings are tied with ribbon. He may slowly make his way down the aisle before or with the flower girl, and should be seated with a relative if he is under four years old. He is not necessarily expected to recess with the bridal party. Usually he and the flower girl steal the show.

TO THE BRIDE'S FATHER:

As the host of your daughter's wedding, most of the expenses of the day will probably fall on your shoulders. (See chapter 4 on budgeting for a complete breakdown of the division of expenses.) This is your chance to make a dream of hers come true. And although she knows that you want to make it as perfect a wedding as possible, one of the most helpful things you can do in the planning stages is to give your wife and the bride-to-be a realistic idea of what you feel is a reasonable amount to spend for that special day. That way they will have some guidelines by which to shop and plan. Your constructive suggestions can be a big help during this time, also.

As the bride-to-be's father, one of your first responsibilities will be to announce officially your daughter's engagement (if there is an announcement party). This over and done with, proper etiquette does not require any other specific duties for you to fulfill until the night before the wedding. Even though the groom's father is responsible for the rehearsal dinner, the bride's father is often asked to offer a word of greeting and/or to share some amusing anecdotes about when his daughter was growing up; or memorable incidents from the bride and groom's courtship.

Then comes the day your daughter has dreamed and planned for. Dress for the bride's father usually consists of either a dark suit or a tuxedo—whichever the bride prefers—decorated with a boutonniere.

The day of the wedding you will be the one to see that the bride gets to the church on time if she is at your home. A few moments alone in the car during the trip to the church will tend to calm nerves and give you an opportunity to share any special thoughts between the two of you. Perhaps rather than driving her yourself, you'd like to ask an usher to drive you both. This is often done. The few moments you will have with your daughter before you escort her down the aisle can also be a special time.

Traditionally, you are honored with "giving the bride away." When asked, "Who gives this woman . . . ," you may respond with either, "I do," or, "Her mother and I do." After kissing the bride you then join your wife to enjoy the rest of the ceremony together.

When the wedding is over you will be an important part of the receiving line. You may also be asked by the bride (ahead of time, of course) to perform other specific duties at the reception, such as introducing the entire wedding party to the guests.

Again, as the host, it is your job to make sure everyone feels welcome. Plan to be the last person to leave the reception so that you can thank all of the guests for coming.

TO THE BRIDE'S MOTHER:

Below is a quick overview of the major responsibilities that will fall to you.
- Before plans for the invitations are finalized, check with the church office to verify the wedding date, time, and the minister's availability.
- Keep an up-to-date calendar of events.
- Hire any extra household or garden help you might need.
- Keep in touch with the groom's parents by inviting them to your home, or sending an occasional note. Also give the bride's father an update of the wedding plans from time to time.
- Let the groom's mother know what you will be wearing to the wedding so she may find an appropriate dress. Also let the groom's father know what the bride's father will be wearing.
- Plan to attend all parties given for the bride to which you are invited.
- Make up a family cookbook containing favorite recipes as a gift for your daughter.
- Help compile the guest list with complete names and addresses.
- Help the bride with final decisions concerning her gown, trousseau, flowers, etc.
- Keep a record of the replies to the wedding invitations.
- Have a notice/invitation put into the church bulletin.
- Cooperate with the groom's family in planning the rehearsal dinner.
- Provide lodging for out-of-town guests and the wedding party.
- Decide how many pews should be reserved for relatives.
- If the wedding is large, have someone take care of the guests' coats.
- Stand first in the receiving line. (Unless other arrangements have been made.)
- Prepare a box lunch for the newlyweds to put in the getaway car.
- Take care of getting the wedding information to the newspaper if you plan to have it printed. Send a copy to the groom's parents.
- Write thank-you notes to everyone who helped you.

If the father is deceased, a male relative or friend may escort the bride in the processional. You, then, may step from your seat to answer the question, "Who gives this woman. . . ." Or, you may escort your daughter down the aisle yourself if you wish; however, this is not usually done.

TO THE GROOM'S FATHER:

You are the host of the rehearsal dinner, and will pay for the expenses of that very special time. It is up to you to say grace before the meal, or arrange for it to be said. A short word of greeting and a salute to the bride and groom is expected, after which the bride's father may do the same.

If you and your wife wish to provide more of the finances for the wedding, you may offer your assistance to the bride or her parents.

There are a few other details to be aware of:
- You may need to assist the groom with his financial obligations in the beginning of their marriage.
- You may be asked to be the best man, if the groom so desires.
- You are part of the receiving line.
- You should dress for the wedding in suitable attire, following the bride's father's lead. You will also be given a boutonniere to wear.

To the Groom's Mother:

After you learn of the engagement, try to arrange a time to meet with the bride's parents to show your approval. If they are from out of town, it is best to write them a letter. It's nice if you can arrange a gathering where relatives and close friends may meet the prospective bride and her parents. A small engagement gift sent to the bride is a nice gesture, too.

You will most likely be invited to a shower given for the bride. Ask her gift preferences, and take her a gift. Two nice gift ideas would be a cookbook of favorite family recipes, and a date book of birthdays and anniversaries, addresses, and phone numbers of the groom's side of the family.

Here are a few other details to be aware of:

- Keep within the number you are allotted for the guest list. If the bride lives far away and the wedding is to be in her town, you might concede some of your allotment so she could invite more friends from nearby. Make sure to get your list to the bride by the date she specifies.
- Send a list of those relatives you know will be attending the wedding so that seating may be arranged.
- If you are from out of town and will need lodging, make arrangements through the bride's mother. Otherwise, contact a hotel yourself. You are expected to pay for your family's lodgings.
- If you live far away from the wedding location, you may honor the bride and groom with a formal reception or open house in your town after the wedding. This will give local family and friends an opportunity to meet the newlyweds.

- You may offer to help address invitations.
- Cooperate in any way you can to assist with the wedding and reception.
- Choose a dress which coordinates with what the bride's mother plans to wear to the wedding.
- Offer to help with the handing out of the corsages and boutonnieres if no one else has done so.
- You may stand in the narthex before the ceremony to greet friends and relatives, especially those from out of town.
- Give a wedding gift of some importance to the newlyweds—perhaps silver, a family heirloom, or money.
- Plan the rehearsal dinner, asking for the bride's counsel.

Note: If either set of parents are divorced, refer to "A Special Word Concerning Divorced Parents" in chapter 19.

To the Bride:

In this book, we have talked about the many responsibilities you have concerning the planning of the wedding. Besides all these, you have a special responsibility to your special friends—your bridesmaids and maid of honor.

Take time to select dresses for them that are attractive and can possibly be worn again. Arrange appropriate times for their fittings, and help them select shoes that are similar in style and color. Tell them what jewelry would be appropriate to wear, or buy it for them. Gifts of hosiery, lipstick, and nail polish are always nice.

Send them a letter from time to time to let them know of the latest details of your plans. This is a good way to let them know what is expected of them, such as when to be there, where to dress, etc.

If any are from out of town, it is your responsibility to arrange lodging for them. Provide for their transportation to the rehearsal, wedding, and reception.

TO THE GROOM:

You have the important part of cooperating with your bride as she manages the plans for this special event. It is a major undertaking. Even if she is able to delegate many responsibilities to others, she will be busy keeping up with the demands on her time. Your attitude of patience and understanding will go a long way toward your future relationship.

You should be involved in such major decisions as setting the date, time, and formality of the wedding and reception. Arrange with your fiancée to visit the minister who will be officiating at your wedding. You should set up any premarital counseling appointments.

Follow your fiancée's instructions on making out a guest list, keeping to the number you are allotted, and giving it to her by the date she's set. You may want to sit down with your family to work this out.

Read through the chapter on budgeting (chapter 4). This will give you a clear idea of some of the other expenses for which you and your family are responsible. Offer to help with more if you are able to and if you know it won't offend the bride's family. It will probably be appreciated.

You may want to purchase your fiancée's engagement ring and wedding ring at the same time. She will probably appreciate having a choice in the selection.

If you like, have them engraved with the wedding date before the wedding.

Decide together with your fiancée on your attendants. The number of guests will determine the number of ushers you will need although you may have as many as you want. But remember that you are responsible for gifts for them and for their accommodations.

Go to several rental shops for your wedding attire. Look closely at the fabric, style, and cut. It is best to try the suit on before renting one. A classic, timeless style will help prevent your photographs from looking dated in the years to come. While you are at the rental shop, arrange for the attire for the best man and ushers as well. If some of your attendants are coming from out of town, send them a measurement card to be returned. By having this card, you will be able to order for them ahead of time.

Begin to look into honeymoon arrangements. Give your bride some choices. You may be eligible for special discounts by planning early. Make all arrangements, and secure tickets and reservations. At the same time, it would be wise to look into your luggage situation, and make arrangements to purchase any needed pieces.

A wedding license must be obtained in the county you and the bride live in, and must be used within sixty days. (This may differ. Check with your local county.)

Be aware of special circumstances before you go to the county office:

- A physician's certificate is required to be signed and dated. It is valid for fifteen days before the wedding. Varying from state to state, it may involve a complete physical or just a premarital examination for VD and a blood test.

The blood work usually takes three to four days.

- If you are under age, a birth certificate as well as your parents' consent are required.
- If any changes occur after you have the marriage license, notify the County Clerk's office.

There are many other details you will need to take care of. The Groom's Checklist in chapter 15 will help you keep everything in order.

TO THE GUESTS:

It is an honor to receive an invitation to a wedding and reception. You have been invited because you have contributed to the life of the bride and/or groom in some way. Therefore, they want to share this occasion with you.

As soon as possible, you should send a note of thanks and your decision to accept or decline the invitation.

Below is an example of a formal acceptance note:

Mr. and Mrs. Robert Anderson
accept with pleasure
the kind invitation
of Mr. and Mrs. Lester Mannly
for
Saturday the 7th of April
at two o'clock
and the reception to follow

If there is an enclosure card with a deadline date, send it immediately. If you are a close friend, you may call the bride's mother to express your happiness and to offer your assistance in any way.

You may accept (or decline) for all the names that were written on the invitation. Remember, only those names written on the inner envelope are invited. If you have small children and their names were not listed, then you can assume they are not invited.

The kind of invitation that is sent will usually indicate the formality of the wedding. If you are in doubt about what to wear, a classic, comfortable street-length dress is always in good taste for a woman. For the man, a business suit or blazer jacket and trousers is suitable.

If you are from out of town, it is expected that you will pay for your overnight accommodations. You may ask the bride's mother to make reservations for you at a nearby hotel. You will need to let her know how many are coming and the type of accommodations you will need. Don't forget to send a check to cover the deposit she will probably have to pay.

On the wedding day, arrive at the church about fifteen minutes before the ceremony is to start. You should be seated soon after the organ begins to play so that you are settled before the relatives are ushered in. (Relatives should be seated ten minutes before the ceremony starts, unless another time has been indicated.)

If you have been sent a pew card, present it to the usher, and he will seat you in the reserved pews. You may tell the usher which side you wish to be seated on (the bride's side traditionally is on the left), but be willing to sit anywhere if the seating has become uneven.

The ushers will offer their right arms to the ladies. If you are a couple and prefer to walk together, you may tell the usher this and then follow him to your seats.

The congregation usually stands (at the

bride's mother's lead) as the bride comes down the aisle. In order to see her, you may turn at an angle and glance to the aisle.

In the receiving line, you will want to shake the hand of the groom and give your best wishes to the bride. Close friends may kiss the bride. Move along so that others may offer their congratulations as well. Offer your name and connection even if you think you are known. Compliment the parents on the wedding, and tell the bride how beautiful she looks.

The guests should go through the receiving line before they have refreshments. In crowded conditions, however, this is not possible. You may join friends or find your way to the punch table.

Gifts

You will need to purchase a gift, and send it to the return address on the wedding invitation envelope. If that is impossible, you may bring it to the reception.

You may call the bride's mother to ask where the bride is registered, or what some of her desires may be. The bride and groom may also be questioned. If their desires are in an expensive category, a group of friends may go together on their request. Think of a way you can add to the enjoyment of their future home, and send your gift as soon as possible.

A selection of a work of art for the bride and groom's home is not recommended. A gift certificate is a better choice. Art shops, as well as other specialty shops, can make these available.

Perhaps you would like to give something that has great worth or sentimental value, such as a treasured antique. If you do this, be sure to include a note with an explanation of its importance to you.

If you are part of an office group and are going together on one gift, you will make the bride happy if you sign it, "from the whole office." This way she will have to write only one thank-you note!

Checks, bonds, and stocks used as gifts should be made out in both the bride's and groom's names. Money is high on the priority list for wedding gifts. Send it ahead to the bride's home, if possible.

CHAPTER EIGHTEEN

The Church Wedding Coordinator

Attention brides!

Do NOT neglect to read this chapter even if your church does not have a church wedding coordinator. The information in this chapter is just as important and relevant to you as that in any of the other chapters. So don't skip over it—read it through!

IF YOUR CHURCH DOESN'T HAVE A WEDDING COORDINATOR

Even if a "professional" wedding coordinator, or hostess, is *not* available, it is to your advantage to appoint someone to that position for your wedding. Often it is a family tradition to ask an aunt to hostess the wedding. If you do not have an aunt or other relative who is experienced with weddings, consider asking a special friend of the family or a woman in the church.

Someone needs to keep things organized and be in charge on the wedding day, and it's nice if it doesn't have to be you. You'll want to focus on the tender moments with your groom and on the friends and relatives who have come to witness such an occasion. So choose someone with whom you can confer dur-

ing the planning stages, and who will be able to carry out your wishes for the day.

Have your hostess read through the wedding rehearsal and wedding day checklists so that she will know what is expected of her. If she is not familiar with the church and its facilities it will be up to you to contact someone who is. (Try the church secretary. She will at least be able to give you the name of someone who can show you the church's wedding provisions.) Set up an appointment and then take this book along with you on the "tour" to fill in the information you'll need (see the form at the end of this chapter).

THE VALUE OF A CHURCH WEDDING COORDINATOR

A good wedding coordinator is invaluable: she saves the bride and her mother from unneeded apprehension; she saves the pastor from excess time at the rehearsal; and she very often saves everyone from a large degree of confusion. She is aware of the church's policies concerning the use of candles, appropriate music, photography, and even any cleanup that is expected. The church wedding coordinator is also familiar with all of the facilities available. She will be acquainted with the sound system, know which rooms are the best dressing rooms, be able to show you the church's wedding provisions (candelabras, kneeling bench, etc.), and inform you as to the kitchen supplies available for a reception. She is a wealth of information; she'll be able to recommend rehearsal dinner sites, caterers, photographers, florists, printers— you name it! And she'll know the quality you can expect because she will have had previous experience with each of them.

And not only can a church wedding coordinator offer you resource lists, she can also provide the rules for proper wedding etiquette. When you initially meet with her, she will most likely bring to mind decisions that you weren't aware you'd have to make!

Besides being your preliminary consultant, another duty of the church wedding coordinator is to supervise the rehearsal. The minister concentrates on guiding the bridal party through the ceremony; but the coordinator instructs everyone as to the mechanics involved (where to stand, when to turn, how to usher, etc.).

You, the bride, are allowed to sit back and make sure that everything is just as you want it to be for the wedding day. All decisions will be finalized. The rehearsal will be very organized, and there will be someone there to whom participants can address any questions they may have.

The goal of the wedding coordinator on the day of the wedding is to relieve the bride from as much apprehension as possible. The coordinator will have a copy of all of the finalized plans, and it will be her sole purpose to see that they are carried out so that the bride can thoroughly

enjoy the wedding of her dreams.

Her goal once the ceremony is completed is to make sure that everyone is happy. Unfortunately, once the ceremony is finished the wedding party often is so carried away in the excitement of the moment that the guests are seemingly forgotten. The job of a wedding coordinator is to see that they do not feel this way. She can view situations objectively, being somewhat removed from both the guests and the wedding party. She will be able to sense when the guests at the end of the receiving line are getting restless, and tactfully suggest that the bride and groom move the people along. Her presence during the formal pictures will remind the participants that the guests are waiting.

Start Something!

So, you can see that the benefits of a church appointing someone to the role of wedding coordinator are obvious. If your church does not have one, consider offering your services. You will have worked through your wedding on your own, and with this book as your guide you will find that you have much to offer other brides-to-be. Whether or not your church is able to pay you for your services, you can be certain that very quickly you will become greatly appreciated. So, start something! Become *your* church's wedding coordinator!

TO THE WEDDING COORDINATOR:

You, as the wedding coordinator, will serve as the liaison between the bride and the church. Many things can be done to help the bride and her mother. They may feel lost in all the details surrounding the upcoming wedding. Your flexible, helpful spirit will be most appreciated.

After the church has cleared the wedding date and the minister has been consulted, the church office will notify you of the wedding. The bride will have been advised to call you to make an appointment. When she does call, verify the date and time of the rehearsal and the wedding, and discuss the need for an organist and/or pianist. You may suggest certain musicians, and remind her to consider the music she wants played before, during, and after the ceremony. (Some churches require that this music be cleared with the minister of music.)

Following this phone conversation, there will be several people you will need to contact:

1. Call the church to verify the date and time on the master calendar.

2. Call the organist to verify the rehearsal and wedding dates, or have an out-of-town organist approved by the minister of music.

3. Make arrangements with the sound system operator to reserve the date of the rehearsal and wedding.

Meeting at the Church

When you meet with the bride, have your resource list of names, phone numbers, and addresses of local photographers, caterers, florists, etc., with you, along with such information as specifics about the church's facilities, any fees, what supplies are available, what supplies need to be purchased, what your duties are, and what the custodian's duties are.

Take the bride for a walk through the church, showing her the various facilities available for her use. Also, show her where the various rooms for dressing are located, and how the reception area can be set up. She may want your advice on the placement in the sanctuary of flowers, greenery, pew bows, and other details in her plans. A Wedding Information Form (included in this chapter) can be used to note the important decisions that are made. The bride should receive a duplicate copy of this.

Discuss the music again at this time. If the bride is using someone other than the church organist, she should have this organist make arrangements with the church office for a key and practice time.

Explain the sound system and who will operate it. If the ceremony is to be taped, discuss the costs involved. Lighting problems will need to be worked out if a video recorder is to be used.

Begin planning the rehearsal, and fill in the Rehearsal Plan, which will ultimately be your guide for the wedding, as much as possible. Stress to the bride the importance of having the rehearsal start on time. Tell her that stand-ins can be used if someone has to be late.

If the reception is to be held at the church, start developing a floor plan for the custodian. (A Custodian's Worksheet can be found in chapter 16.) Discuss with the bride who will dispose of the flowers and decorations when the event is over.

It's a nice idea to go out for breakfast or lunch with the bride and her mother after meeting at the church. This way you will become better acquainted.

WEDDING INFORMATION FORM

Church _____ Phone _____

Wedding coordinator _____ Phone _____

Bride _____ Phone _____ (home)

_____ (work)

Groom _____ Phone _____ (home)

_____ (work)

Wedding date _____ Time _____

Number of guests expected _____

Pastor(s) _____ Phone _____

_____ _____

Bride, groom, or either set of parents members or

regular attenders? _____

Fees paid? _____

Rehearsal date _____ Time _____

Will both sets of parents be present? _____

Dress _____

Organist _____ Phone _____

Other _____ Phone _____

Vocalist(s) _____ Phone _____

_____ _____

Other musicians _____ Phone _____

_____ _____

Music selections approved? _____

Number of music stands _____

Number of folders _____

Sound system operator _____ Phone _____

Taped? _____ Video recorded? _____

Microphones _____

Photographer _____ Phone _____

Florist _____ Phone _____

WEDDING INFORMATION FORM (cont.)

Color scheme of wedding _____

Length of center aisle _____

Number of pews _____

Number of windows _____

Time florist arrives _____

Time photographer arrives _____

Time wedding party arrives:

      Women _____   Men _____

        ____ dress at home   ____ dress at home

        ____ dress at church   ____ dress at church

            room ____   room ____

Pictures to be taken when? _____

   of whom? _____

Church items to be used:

      ____ candelabra(s)   ____ podium for guest book

      ____ unity candelabra   ____ gift table

      ____ kneeling bench   ____ candlelighters (torches)

      ____ other: ____ candles (number ____)

Items to bring to rehearsal (bride):

      ____ ribbon bouquets   ____ checks for musicians, etc.

      ____ wedding shoes   ____ license

      ____ programs   ____ rice

      ____ maps   ____ cake knife and server

      ____ guest book and pen   ____ snack for wedding day

      ____ tape (cassette)   ____ gowns/tuxedos

      ____ other:

Guest book attendant _____

Gift table attendant _____

Host and hostess _____

Responsible for locking gifts in car _____

WEDDING INFORMATION FORM (cont.)

Time music begins _____

Candlelighting
Time   Which Ones   Who
_____   *Windows*   _____
_____   *Candelabras*   _____
_____   *Christ candle*   _____
_____   *Other*   _____

Ushering (special)
Time   Who   Usher
_____   _____   _____
_____   _____   _____
_____   _____   _____
_____   _____   _____
_____   *Mother and father of groom*
_____   *Mother of bride*   _____

Aisle runner: Time _____ Usher(s) _____
Aisle to be used _____

Maid of honor _____
Bridesmaids _____
_____
_____

Other _____
Processional: ___ single ___ with groomsmen

Best man _____
Groomsmen _____
Ushers _____
_____

Other _____
Processional: ___ single ___ with bridesmaids
Bride: Blusher veil? _____ Who will lift it? _____
        When? _____
Roses for mothers? _____ When given? _____

WEDDING INFORMATION FORM (cont.)

Recessional order:

Candles extinguished: When? _____ Usher(s) _____

_____

Ushering (special)
  Who   Usher
  Parents of bride _____
  Parents of groom _____
_____
_____
_____

How are guests dismissed? _____

_____

Receiving line order:

____ Reception to be held at church
     Date and facilities cleared with church office? _____

Caterer or person in charge _____
    Phone _____

Bakery _____ Phone _____

Reception hostess _____

Who is responsible to clean up? _____

_____

Special bouquet to throw? _____
    Garter? _____

Other:

REHEARSAL PLAN

TIME

_____ Church open—set up

_____ Florist arrives

_____ Bridal party arrives

_____ Photographer arrives

_____ Bridal party in sanctuary (if pictures are to be taken)

_____ _____

_____ _____

_____ _____

_____ _____

_____ Music begins

_____ Candles lighted

_____ Special ushering—parents prepare to be seated

_____ _____

_____ _____

_____ _____

_____ _____

_____ Mother of the groom followed by father

_____ Mother of the bride

_____ Aisle runner

_____ Solo—Bride and attendants prepare for processional
              Groom and attendants in vestry

_____ Processional

_____ Marriage Service

_____ Recessional

_____ Receiving line order:

Before the Rehearsal

Walk through the plans with the bride. It is preferable to do this at the church on the day of the rehearsal. This meeting will insure that the rehearsal runs smoothly. The bride can feel confident knowing she has gone over the details and that everything is to her liking.

Using the Rehearsal Plan, go over again what times the various events are to occur. Review the details concerning those who are to be ushered in at special times and by whom. Note any changes that have occurred since your last meeting. It may be wise for you to call the florist, photographer, bakery, and caterer to verify arrangements.

By this time the bride will be in control of many things that had not been worked out previously. Offer to help with any last-minute details. Your job is to put together her plans for the rehearsal. The main thing you can do for the bride is to listen to her; give her your undivided attention and support.

Here are some miscellaneous details to be aware of:

- Purchase a 7″ x 9″ or other suitable notebook for instructions, checklists, duties, and resources.
- Maintain an "emergency kit" just for weddings. Purchase a carry-all bag and outfit it with the following:

Thread (selection of colors), needles, pins, (variety of sizes and kinds)
Shirt buttons
Thimble
Pin cushion

Scissors (for cutting metal, paper, or cloth)

Nail file and emery board
Nail polish

Hair spray
Bobby and hair pins
Comb, mirror

Talcum powder
Tissues

Breath mints
Aspirin
Antacid
Small first aid kit
Capsule of ammonia

Static cling spray
Lint clothes brush
Cleaning fluid

Pen, pencil
Plain envelopes, name tags

All-purpose glue, cellophane tape, masking tape

Matches

Tape measure

Other:

- Plan on dressing nicely for the wedding, with no intention of stealing the show. You are not part of the wedding party.
- Wear *comfortable* dress shoes, so you are able to move quickly.
- Wear a name badge that states your name and role. This will allow people to recognize you as a representative of the church.

WEDDING COORDINATOR REHEARSAL CHECKLIST

BEFORE:
- Make out name tags for everyone if the group is large and they all do not know each other.
- Make an agenda for yourself and for anyone else listed on the Rehearsal Plan. Otherwise, only provide one each for the organist, minister, soloist, and sound operator.
- Write out the directions for the rehearsal.
- You may need to mark the places where the attendants are to stand with small pieces of masking tape on the sanctuary floor.

ARRIVE EARLY

MEET THE ORGANIST
- Agree on the time the prelude will start and cues for the soloist and processional.
- Ask him to play an excerpt from the beginning and ending of each accompaniment during the rehearsal so the participants will know how the music fits into the wedding.
- Discuss a possible selection for ushering in the mothers if one has not previously been decided on.
- Give him an agenda.
- Mention that brief periods of silence are often effective.

MEET THE SOLOIST
- Ask him to sing or play excerpts from only the beginning and ending of the selection(s) during the rehearsal.
- Agree on cues and where to stand or sit.
- Ask if he needs a music stand or folder, and discuss the need for a microphone if the service is being taped.
- Give him an agenda.

MEET THE MINISTER
- Agree on the cues for the processional.
- Give him an agenda.
- Review any unusual procedures or changes just made.

MEET THE SOUND OPERATOR
- Agree on cues.
- Give him an agenda.

TALK WITH BEST MAN
- If he does not have it with him, remind him to bring the wedding license partially completed to the wedding.

TALK WITH USHERS
- Remind them to prelight the candles at some time for better results on the wedding day.

- Instruct them concerning their responsibilities. (See pages 152-154.)

TALK WITH BRIDE AND GROOM
- If they are having pictures taken before the ceremony, show them the place where they may meet alone for a few minutes.

Final Instructions for the Rehearsal

1. Ask if anyone will need a wake-up call. Arrange for that.
2. Eat something before coming.
3. Time to arrive at church.
4. Reminder of transportation to the church for bride and groom.
5. Location of dressing rooms for ladies and men.
6. If men are dressing at home, bring coat on hanger to avoid wrinkles. Check tux and shirt sizes before dressing to be sure they're not mixed up.
7. Location of rest rooms.
8. Lock clothes and valuables in the trunk of car. (May use shopping bags.)
9. Where to receive flowers (bouquets, corsages, boutonnieres). Someone to assist.
10. Photographer's schedule and locations.
11. Ushers in narthex forty-five minutes before the wedding. Please do not leave after that.
12. Time sanctuary should be clear for guests.
13. Snack time. (If pictures are taken before the wedding.)
14. Mothers should carry small purses or place in the pew ahead of time.
15. Ask to have relatives or anyone receiving flowers introduce themselves to you.

WEDDING AGENDA (Fill out and copy for participants if programs are not available)

Wedding of _____ Date _____ Time _____

TIME

_____ Church open

_____ Florist arrives

If reception at church
Caterer arrives:
Bakery delivery:

_____ Wedding party arrives

_____ Photographer arrives (guest book attendant, gift attendant, sound operator, musicians)

_____ Pictures in sanctuary (if taken ahead of time)

_____ Snack time (optional)

_____ Ushers in narthex (45 min. before ceremony)

_____ Organ begins to play—ushering begins   Reserved rows:

_____ Candles lighted

_____ Groom's parents arrive (5-10 minutes before ceremony, 30 minutes if greeting)

_____ Special ushering: Usher

              1.

              2.

              3.

              4.

_____ Attendants ready and waiting

_____ Mother of the groom *followed by father*

_____ Mother of the bride (can be seated the hour of the wedding)

_____ Aisle runner

_____ Solo (optional)

_____ Bride and father ready (can be at the hour of the wedding)

_____ Processional

Recessional

Ushering:

Receiving line order:

16. Emergency kit—explain where it will be located and what it contains (needle and thread, breath mints, hair spray and clips, etc.).
17. Remind the bridal party not to lock their legs when standing during the ceremony. Stand relaxed, on one foot and then on the other. Circulation may be cut off otherwise and cause dizziness or fainting. Rather than closing eyes during prayers, lower lids if there is a tendency to feel dizzy. Blacking out is like tunnel vision. Things begin to appear closer together and further away. If this happens, kneel! The blood will rush to the head and you will feel better. If someone does faint, help him to the front seat. He will come to. In the meantime, the wedding will go on!
18. Give order of the receiving line.
19. Announcements for order of the reception.
20. Time the church will be locked after the wedding.
21. Ask the bride, minister, mother if there are any other instructions.
22. Tell them that you will be there to give them their cues and to help in any way you can. Thank them for their cooperation.

Receiving line instructions:
Introduce yourself if you don't know a guest. The person will probably take the hint and offer his or her name in return. Smile at everyone, shake hands, and say just a few words of welcome. (You may want to take off any rings on your right hand to avoid a painful handshake.) Present each guest to the person standing next to you. Everyone should stay in the receiving line until the last guests have greeted the bride and groom.

Wedding Day Checklist for the Wedding Coordinator

Arrive early.

Unlock any facilities that you are responsible for.

Meet the florist:
Double-check list provided by the bride to see that all of the flowers and decorations have been delivered.

Meet the photographer:
Remind him of the rules of the church, and the time he is to be out of the sanctuary if the pictures are being taken before the wedding. Give him a program.

Meet with sound operator:
Check proper setup of sound equipment, see that he has the tape for the recording, and give him a program.

Give programs, double-check cues, and synchronize watches with:
Pastor(s)
Organist
Soloist
Other musicians

Candlelighters:
Wicks trimmed or replaced if needed
Matches

Double-check:
Preparation of sanctuary
Rest rooms, dressing rooms
Temperature control, fans
Lighting

Set up:
Guest book and pen, if used at the church
Programs
Cellophane tape to attach cards to gifts
Emergency kit
Pitcher of water and cups in vestry

Have the mother or bride, upon arrival, check the decorations and flowers to see that they are the way that they ordered them.

Assist bride, if needed, with dressing, adjusting veil, etc. (Many girls have personal attendants to do this.)

Assist with flowers, pinning on corsages and boutonnieres, etc. (Remember, stems down!) This must be completed before pictures are taken. Someone else may be asked to do this—someone who knows many of the people in the wedding.

Have an agenda on hand for cues.

Give final instructions to the ushers (or head usher):
Cues to: Light candles
        Escort special guests
        Escort mothers
        Lay aisle runner
        Begin ushering after
            recessional

Close the guest book before the wedding if a long line is forming.

Remind little children to use the bathroom before the processional.

Line up wedding party for processional and give cues to enter sanctuary. (Someone else may be assigned to do this duty.)

Arrange bride's train. Try to stay out of the way of the photographer.

Close doors, direct late guests to side aisles.

Check with the reception hostess if reception is to be held at the church.

Guide the ushers after the recessional.

Arrange the receiving line, if necessary. Check with the bride and her mother for any needs. Possibly take cups of punch on a tray for the bridal party.

After the wedding:
See that the candles have been snuffed out. (Some brides ask to keep the candles. They can be put back in the original boxes.)

Replace the candlelighter (torch) wicks for the next wedding.

Check for lost-and-found items in church and dressing rooms.

Remain on premises until the building is cleared and lock facilities that you are responsible for.

Other:
If a boutonniere is missing or damaged, take a flower from one of the bridesmaids' bouquets or from a large corsage.

If pictures are still being taken when guests arrive, ask them to kindly wait outside if it is a nice day.

An insect repellent spray may be used outside the premises, if needed.

Blockades for street closings may often be procured from the city for a period of time during the wedding. They are brought by a city truck, put in place by ushers, and picked up later.

THE WEDDING COORDINATOR'S MASTER WEDDING RECORD									
DATE	TIME	REHEARSAL	NAME	PHONE	P.A./ORGANIST	COORDINATOR/HOSTESS	PASTOR	RECEPTION LOCATION	

CHURCH FACILITIES

When the church does not provide the services of a wedding coordinator, enlist the church secretary or someone familiar with the facilities to assist you with the checklist. Ask to be taken on a walk around the church, if possible.

CHURCH _____

PHONE _____

ADDRESS _____

MINISTER _____

CUSTODIAN _____

ORGANIST _____

SECRETARY _____

SOUND OPERATOR _____

OTHER _____

Inquire regarding:
 Rules, regulations, and permissions
  Musical selections
  Outside musicians
  Photographs (flash allowed during ceremony?)
  Rice, bird seed, confetti
  Flowers and greens, rose petals
  Fire laws (candles, smoking)
  Church capacity
  Sound system (cassettes?)
  Mode of dress (sleeve length, neckline, hemline)
  Use of tacks or tape on pews
  Aisles to be used
  Parking, closing of street with barricades
  Communion
 Facilities available for wedding
  Candelabra
  Christ candle
  Aisleabra
  Number of pews
  Hurricane shades
  Number of windows
  Candleholders
  Candlelighters (torches)
  Kneeling bench, cushions, or prie-dieu
  Aisle runner
  Length of aisle
  Podium or table for guest book
  Table for gifts
  Coat racks
 Rooms for dressing
  Mirror
  Cloak rack
  Table
  Chairs
 Lighting (dimmers, spots)
Supplies furnished or that need to be purchased or rented
 Candles
 Other
Sound system equipment
 Cost involved
  Tapes
Organ, other instruments (piano, chimes, bells)
 Fee
 Repairing and tuning
Custodian duties
 Cleaning
  Sanctuary before and after wedding
  Reception room before and after wedding
  Washrooms, dressing rooms
 Temperature control
  Opening and closing of windows and doors
  Regulation of fans, lighting
 Setting up and taking down of wedding facilities
 Clearing of sidewalks, steps, and parking area
 Disposal of trash
 Fee, gratuity
Air conditioning, heat

Reception room facilities
- Tables
    - Buffet
    - Dining
    - Cake
    - Gift
    - Guest book
- Chairs, number available
- Table linens, napkins
- Dinnerware, silverware
- Coffee maker
- Coffee and tea service
- Punch bowls, cups, ladle
- Candleholders
- Coat racks
- Dishwasher
    - Soap, towels

Refrigerator, freezer
Trash containers
Place for caterer's equipment and instrument cases of musicians
Lighting, fans
Rules regarding decorations, alcohol, smoking, candles
Electrical outlets

FEE FOR USE OF CHURCH _____

RECEPTION HOSTESS _____

APPOINTMENT WITH MINISTER _____

PREMARITAL COUNSELING _____

POLICE OFFICER FOR TRAFFIC CONTROL _____

The Rehearsal

AN OVERVIEW

It is important to plan the rehearsal as carefully as you have the wedding. If you have the services of a church wedding coordinator (as discussed in the previous chapter) or a hostess, she will assist you after you have made your plans with the minister. If possible, it would be wise to walk through all the details the morning of the rehearsal.

The rehearsal is usually set for the day or evening before the wedding and held at the wedding site. The out-of-town participants should arrive by this time. The rehearsal will involve the entire wedding party including both sets of parents, the minister, the organist, vocalist(s), any other musicians, and both families. (Others can join you for the rehearsal dinner, if you wish.) It will usually take an hour to an hour and a half to gather everyone together, rehearse, and have the final instructions.

It would be best to send cards to everyone to advise them of the date, time, place, and directions to the location. It's a good idea even to call them the day before to remind them and to see if there are any problems with this arrangement. If you are going to a formal restaurant for the dinner afterward, let everyone know

how to dress for the occasion (generally men in sports jackets, women in dresses, etc.).

The rehearsal is divided into three parts: procedures, ceremony (which you plan with the minister), and instructions to the ushers.

The person in charge, usually the officiating minister, will gather everyone together for a few opening remarks and prayer. He may ask you and your groom to introduce your parents, the attendants, and all other participants so everyone can get acquainted. Instructions will then be given (by the wedding coordinator) concerning the formal, organized parts of the wedding. A system of cues needs to be worked out between the organist and minister.

You are basically the one in charge of all the arrangements. The minister and wedding coordinator are there simply to help you carry them out. So you will be asked to give your approval of the overall appearance. If you want to make any changes, the rehearsal is the time to do it.

Next, the pastor will proceed with the rehearsal of the ceremony which you have planned with him and your groom. As the ushers are not needed at this time, the coordinator can give them their instructions off to one side. Otherwise, they can be instructed later. The ushers will need to practice their individual duties separately.

When the minister has finished with the rehearsal of the ceremony, you and your attendants may recess to the back of the church while the men go to the vestry to wait for the beginning of the processional. The parents should follow you back also. (The ushers will be instructed at this time if it has not been done before.)

The rehearsal of the entire wedding will then begin with the ushering in of the mothers to their places. It will continue, with excerpts of the music, until the mothers are ushered out. You may wish to practice the processional again. The wedding coordinator will give you your cues for entering the sanctuary.

After the rehearsal of the wedding is finished, you may also practice the receiving line if you wish. Everyone should then return to the front of the church to receive final instructions.

With these orderly proceedings, you will notice the enjoyment of the rehearsal is not lost in confusion. This will also allow the rehearsal to be completed in a short time.

PREPARING FOR THE REHEARSAL: DECISIONS TO BE MADE

Miscellaneous

1. How should everyone dress for the rehearsal? Casual, or semidressy for the dinner afterward?
2. Who will give the cues?
3. What is the time schedule for the rehearsal?
4. What announcements will need to be made at the end of the rehearsal regarding the wedding day?
5. What aisle(s) will be used? (If there is not a center aisle, the processional is usually on the left and the recessional on the right.)

Candlelighting

The candlelighting may be done by one or two ushers, or by specially designated people. Lighting the candles, the lowest to the highest, should be synchronized. Each person should watch the other out of the corner of his eye. It should be done slowly. If for some reason a candle doesn't light right away, one usher should wait for the other. To prevent lighting problems, briefly prelight each candle the night before. This way if there is wax on any of the wicks, it will be removed. Also, you may then replace any faulty candles.

The lighting of the three-branch Christ candelabra is a meaningful act and should be rehearsed as part of the ceremony. It symbolizes the unity between the bride and groom, between the two families, and the union with Christ.

The two outer candles can be lit any of the following ways:

1. Ushers light them when the other candelabra are lighted.
2. The mothers, fathers, or both go to the front to light the candle on their side. (They can do this before they are seated, or rise afterward and do it.) After lighting the candle, your father would go back to join you for the processional, while your mother and the groom's parents take their seats.
3. Another member from each family may light the candles.

If you choose to have both sets of parents light the outside candles you will need to arrange ahead of time where they will pick up the special lighters used for this purpose and how they will light them (usually from one of the candelabras).

The mother should precede the father when going up to light the candle. She should rest her hand on his arm as he lights the candle. If there are any steps they will have to descend on their way back, the father might go first if there are only a few steps. He would then turn to the mother, holding his hand out for her as she descended. Otherwise, they should descend together, he assisting her.

Write your decisions in the space below:

Which candles	When to light	Who will light
Windows		
Candleabra		
Christ candelabra		

Music

Send the musicians a duplicate list of the selections to be played, in the order they are to be played. Include the date and time of the rehearsal and the wedding, and your phone number. At the rehearsal ask them to sing or play excerpts only. Practice should be done on their own time.

Before the night of the rehearsal, consider the following questions:

1. What selections will you use, and what order should they be in?
2. Should the soloist be in view or out of view? Will he or she need a folder or music stand?
3. Will you have any special musicians performing at the reception?

Ushering

Decide who will usher in the mothers and any special relatives you want to honor.

(It may be the head usher, a son, the groom, a father, etc.)

The Mother of the Bride is the last person to be ushered in. She may choose to (1) go in at the time the wedding is set to start, (2) go in a few minutes before so that the processional may start at the exact time, or (3) wait to be ushered in until she feels that all the guests have arrived. However, those guests who arrive early may wonder what is detaining the processional.

It is her privilege to sit on the aisle at the wedding, but she may choose to take the second seat in, leaving a place for your father.

Use the space below to note any special arrangements:

Special guests	Which usher	Time

Aisle Runner

The aisle runner is made of a heavy sail cloth or a plastic fabric. It can be rented from the florist, or from the church if it has one. It is either folded at the base of the steps or rolled up, with a handle. It can be pulled by one or two people and is to be drawn back after the mothers have been seated, before you and your father walk down the aisle. (The other alternative is to have it tacked down ahead of time, in which case no guests may be seated from that aisle.)

Unrolling the runner often becomes the most precarious task of the ushers, because it cannot be practiced beforehand. Be sure they are aware of how it should be done (see chapter 16 under "The Ushers"). Care should be taken to pull it as straight as possible and not to jerk it loose from where it is fastened in front. It should be pulled to its full length and smoothed down in the vestibule.

Determine ahead of time which ushers will pull it back and when they should do this.

Processional
Groomsmen
1. Where will they enter from, and where will they stand once at the front?
2. How should they enter: single file, in pairs, or up the aisle with the bridesmaids as couples?

Bridesmaids
1. How should they walk in: with a natural, easy walk, or with the hesitation step? (This step is done by keeping the weight on the forward foot and sliding the back foot forward with the music. For balance, keep feet slightly apart, and do not try to walk a chalk line. Take small steps.)
2. Should their order for walking down the aisle be based on height, or status?
3. If there are many bridesmaids, should they walk in one at a time, or in pairs?
4. Will the junior bridesmaids go in first, or right before you?
5. If there is both a maid of honor and a matron of honor, how will they walk in for the processional and out for the recessional: individually or as a pair?

Ring Bearer and Flower Girl
1. Should they walk in together, or will the ring bearer go first?
2. After reaching the front, should they stand with the rest of the party, sit in the first pew, or join their families?

Bride
1. When walking in with your father, will you take his right or left arm? (It is generally best to take his right arm if your dress has a train. That way he will not have to step around—or on!—your dress.)
2. Will you present each set of parents with a rose? If so, will you give it to your parents before the ceremony, and his parents after, or will you give the roses at the same time?
3. Will you wear a blusher veil over your face until the groom kisses you?

Recessional
1. Should the flower girl and/or ring bearer be a part of the recessional? If so, should they walk out separately or as a pair?
2. Should the candles be extinguished before the guests are dismissed? If so, by whom?
3. How should the guests be dismissed: ushers indicate row by row, or exit at random by themselves?

Items to Obtain
- Candelabra
- Kneeling bench or prie-dieu
- Podium for guest book
- Gift table
- Candlelighters (torches)
- Other:

ITEMS TO BRING TO THE REHEARSAL
___ Ribbon bouquets from bridal showers
___ Wedding shoes to practice processional
___ Printed programs or copies of the agenda
___ Guest book and pen
___ Any recording material you are responsible for (cassette)
___ Checks for musicians

____ Honorarium for minister

____ Wedding license, already filled in

____ Your gown, the bridesmaids' dresses, and the groomsmen's tuxedos, if they can be locked away overnight

____ Rice pouches

____ Snack of orange juice, crackers, etc., for wedding day

____ Copies of map to rehearsal dinner, if needed

____ Attendants' gifts, if given at rehearsal dinner

____ Copies of map to reception

____ Other (candles, paper napkins, plates, cake knife/server, etc.)

Remember: The more you bring the night of the rehearsal, the less you'll have to forget on the wedding day.

The Wedding Day

Before we actually talk about the events of the day, just a word about how you feel on this day could be of help. In approaching the wedding ceremony, the proper attitude makes a big difference. First, the wedding is a sacred time of worship. During this time you and your groom offer joint praise to God for bringing the two of you together. It is a time for you to commit your lives to one another and to God's glory; so it is a solemn day. But solemn does not mean joyless, and sacred does not mean no smiles. A wedding is a time of great joy. Our Lord Jesus agreed with this when, at the wedding in Cana of Galilee, he saved the best wine until last. Wine is symbolic of joy.

Both you and your groom should attempt to approach the rehearsal and wedding ceremony in a relaxed manner. An overly perfectionistic couple will surely find something to be disappointed about. Anything could go wrong at your wedding—the soloist could forget a line, Dad may not be able to say "I do," the flower girl could freeze up and refuse to go down the aisle, a bridesmaid may pass out. Just remember if one of these things does happen, most likely in the years to come it will become one of your most cherished memories. Do your best to plan a beauti-

ful ceremony that is glorifying to God, and then RELAX. Attempt to be in a state of mind in which you can enjoy yourself. Enjoy the bridesmaids walking down the aisle, the music you have specially chosen for the day, the flickering of the candles, how your mother looks—and especially the face of your beloved.

THE SCHEDULE

The wedding day can be exciting, emotional . . . and hectic. This special day will need to have a time schedule all its own. To make a time schedule for this last day, start by deciding what time your mother should be seated at the church. Next, note the time you want to arrive at the church (this may already have been determined by the photographer). Also consider the time you need to leave on your honeymoon. These are pivotal points for your day. Use these times to determine the rest of the day's schedule.

If you are dressing into your gown at home, your plans will need to reflect this. Allow time for bathing when you first get up, and then have breakfast. There may be several miscellaneous errands to run and some last-minute items to pack, etc., so schedule accordingly. Allow time for fixing your makeup and hair, and putting on your wedding dress. Then you're ready for any photography that is to be done at your home. After the photographs are taken, you should be on your way to the church.

BRIDE'S WEDDING DAY PLANNER

If dressing at home:
Time
_____ Get up, bathe/shampoo
_____ Breakfast, prayer time
_____ Miscellaneous (last-minute packing and errands, etc.)
_____ Makeup, dressing, hair
_____ Photography
_____ Drive to church
_____ Arrive at church
_____ Snacktime and relax
_____ Mother of bride seated
_____ Processional

If dressing at church:
Time
_____ Arise, bathe/shampoo, dress in casual clothes
_____ Breakfast, prayer time
_____ Miscellaneous (last-minute packing and errands, etc.)
_____ Drive to church
_____ Bridal party arrives

Church to be open _____
Florist to arrive _____
If reception is at church:
   Bakery _____
   Rental Service _____
   Caterer _____
   Assistants _____
(Bride checks arrangements.)

_____ Photographer arrives
_____ Dressed and ready for pictures
   Order of pictures:

_____ Snacktime and relax
_____ Mother of bride seated
_____ Processional

Write below the following reception items in the order you plan to do them.

receiving line   eat   announce the wedding party
photographs   throw the bouquet   other
cut the cake   throw the garter   leave
1.   4.   7.
2.   5.   8.
3.   6.   9.

Order for after the wedding and reception:

If you are dressing at the church, your morning schedule will be similar to that mentioned above: bathing, breakfast, and miscellaneous errands. However, you will leave for the church much sooner. When you arrive at the church, try to check such details as: Is the church set up the way you want? Has the florist come? If so, have the flowers been put where you want them? If the reception is held at the church, check those details as well (tables, caterer, helpers, etc.).

As soon as the bridal party arrives they should begin dressing into their wedding attire. The photographer will either be taking shots of you dressing, or he may be setting up for formal pictures in the sanctuary. Everyone should gather at the specified time for the necessary pictures. Afterward, relax in a side room and munch on the crackers and orange juice you brought to the rehearsal.

A SAMPLE WEDDING

Perhaps the following sample wedding will help you determine the time frame for your own. It is only a suggestion as to how the day might proceed, but use it as a guide, feeling free to add your own unique touches.

About forty-five minutes before the wedding, the ushers should be in the narthex with their boutonnieres pinned on. They should check the candlelighters and be sure they have matches. They are there to greet early guests and to run any last-minute errands.

A half hour before the wedding, the organist will begin to play the prelude softly. Two of the ushers will light the candlelighters and then light the candles in the windows and in the chancel. (No part of the Christ candelabra should be lit at this time.) The ushers will then extinguish their lighters, leave them in the front pews, and return to the back by the side aisles.

After this, other ushers may begin escorting the guests to their seats using the center aisle.

The groom's parents will be greeting friends from out of town in the narthex, while the bride, her attendants, the flower girl, ring bearer, the bride's parents, and possibly grandparents wait in a private room. The minister, groom, best man, and other attendants will wait in the vestry.

Between ten and five minutes before the wedding, the close family members will be seated in the reserved pews with the grandparents seated last, in the third pew.

Then, a few minutes before the hour of the wedding, the mother of the groom will be escorted by the head usher to the second pew on the right-hand side of the aisle. The father of the groom will follow and be seated beside her.

At the hour of the wedding, the bride's mother will be ushered to the second pew on the left-hand side of the aisle, with the bride's father following and being seated with his wife. The bride's mother and the groom's parents will watch the bride's father for the sign to go up and light the Christ candelabra. (Read the section on candlelighting in chapter 19 to get a clear idea of what could happen at this point.)

A special musical number will be played as the parents light these candles. After they have been seated, two ushers will come forward to take the corners of the aisle runner, which is at the base of the stairs. The bride's father will slip back to the narthex while this is going on.

After the runner has been drawn completely out, a vocal solo selection is presented. During this solo, everyone will take their places in the narthex and in the vestry in preparation for the processional. The ushers will quickly make their way to the vestry during this solo.

After the solo, there will be a pause as the organist prepares for the processional. The door to the vestry will open when the fanfare is played. The minister will come in and take his place in the center while the groom takes his place in front of the first pew on the right. The best man and the groomsmen stand next to him, one pace from each other. All will be turned halfway, facing the back of the sanctuary with arms relaxed at their sides.

At this point, the first bridesmaid begins the procession. She will walk slowly with short comfortable steps. When she has gone about two-thirds of the distance, the next bridesmaid will start. This continues with the others following in the same manner. The ring bearer and flower girl will follow the maid of honor. When the maid of honor has reached her place, the organ sounds another fanfare. The bride enters the sanctuary on her father's arm. When she enters, the minister will nod to her mother so that she will stand. The entire congregation follows her example so as to honor this occasion.

Both the bride and her father will start the walk on the left foot. She will take her father's arm so that he can leave her at the front without having to step around her train. When they arrive at the front, the minister will ask, "Who gives this woman to be married to this man?" The father will answer, "Her mother and I," and then kiss the bride. (He may pull back her blusher at this time.) She will then move up to her groom while her father joins her mother. The bride will transfer her bouquet from her right hand to her left when she takes her groom's arm. The minister will give the bride's mother a nod to be seated, and the congregation will be seated also.

The maid of honor will hand her bouquet to the next bridesmaid so that she is free to hold the bride's bouquet, arrange her train, help with her veil, etc. Then she and the best man will ascend the steps to the altar before the bride and groom so that they will not disturb her train. As the bride and groom ascend, he will hold her elbow as she slightly lifts her skirt. The other attendants will turn gradually, facing the bride and groom as they do this. Once they are at the altar, the bride will hand her bouquet to the maid of honor.

The minister will lead them through the ceremony as rehearsed. When it is time to descend, the bride will take her bouquet back from the maid of honor, hold her skirt with one hand, and be assisted down by the groom. At the bottom of the stairs, they will pause for a moment, the bride will take her husband's arm, adjust her bouquet, and then joyfully walk to the narthex.

The recessional will be done in the reverse of the processional, except that the attendants will walk out as couples. The maid of honor will take the best man's arm, descend the steps, take her bouquet from the bridesmaid, and recess. The ring bearer and flower girl will then walk together to the back. The other attendants should stand in place until it is their turn to recess. They will not move up all at once, as though waiting in a ticket line. But one by one they will move to the center and leave the sanctuary.

When the recessional is completed, two ushers will come to the front. They will stop by the parents' pews, and one will nod to the bride's parents first. They will rise and walk out together as the usher leads the way up the aisle. The other usher immediately nods to the groom's parents. They will then rise and walk together behind their usher.

The ushers will then return to escort the elderly relatives up the aisle. When they return from this, two ushers will extinguish the candles. They will then turn and direct the guests as they leave row by row, one side and then the other, beginning with the bride's side. Attention will be given to the timing since the receiving line is being held in the narthex. The ushers will let the guests out slowly to prevent a bottleneck at the back of the sanctuary. Anyone who must leave in a hurry can exit another way.

TRANSPORTATION

The ushers could be responsible for chauffeuring you and your father to the church, and later you and the groom to the reception. Usually the ushers also arrange transportation for the bridesmaids from the wedding to the reception. The best man often chauffeurs the bride and groom.

It is not unheard of to rent one or more limousines for transporting the bridal party to the church and reception. This is particularly desirable if parking facilities are limited. If four limousines are rented, one should go to the groom's home for him and the best man. The other three should go to your home if the bridesmaids have gathered there. The bridesmaids ride in one, your mother and a close friend in another, and you and your father in the last. The limousines should wait at the church during the ceremony to transport you and the groom to the reception. The other three will transport the maid of honor and best man, one or both sets of parents, and the bridesmaids.

Out-of-town guests may be assigned a person to pick them up or to lead the way if they have their own cars. Someone should be available to direct them or assist them in finding their way home.

All assigned drivers should be given:

- a list of the people they're responsible for
- what time to be where
- specific addresses of the church, reception, homes
- maps, if necessary, and
- any written instructions.

A SPECIAL WORD CONCERNING DIVORCED PARENTS

If your parents or the groom's parents are divorced, they are free to sit or stand together if they care to. However, it may be confusing to the guests.

After your mother has been escorted to the front pew, her spouse may sit beside her. Your father would sit two rows behind her with his spouse. A fiancé would not sit in the family area but would take a seat further back.

CHAPTER TWENTY ONE

The Reception

The reception is a time of celebration. After a radiant marriage ceremony, you gather with your guests to share your excitement. It is a time of letting your guests know how much you appreciate their presence on this special day.

The reception may be as elaborate or as simple as you desire. There is a great deal of variation between the "marathon" reception and the reception that consists of a handshake, glass of punch, and a piece of cake. But either direction you take, your goal should be to create an atmosphere of giving and love. It will be best to do this in the style of entertaining to which you are accustomed. But let your imagination and creativity run free as the arrangements are made.

TYPES OF RECEPTIONS

The ultraformal reception should take place at a hotel or club. It would begin with a receiving line and punch, followed by a full-course meal served by waiters. All the tables for the bridal party, parents, and guests would be designated by place cards or table numbers. Music and decorations would be expected.

At a formal or semiformal reception, the proceedings would be the same, but on a less grand level. There would be place cards for a sit-down dinner. Or, if it's a buffet reception, the tables could be set or the silverware could be picked up at the buffet table, and the guests could be seated randomly.

A reception in the church "parlor" or fellowship hall contains many of the elements of a formal reception. It loses some of the formality, however, if there is a lack of space. An afternoon reception could be considered a "tea" with appropriate sandwiches and cake. In the evening, more substantial food is generally served, such as hot and cold hors d'oeuvres, cake, and punch.

A reception in someone's home can be pleasant, too, especially after a small, informal wedding. To give you a better idea of the space you will need, consider that a 14' x 35' room will hold about forty people for a stand-up reception. When there are too many people, there is not enough room to move about, and some of the guests may never reach the buffet table. Removing some of the furniture might be a good idea, but takes away from the general warmth the home affords.

DECORATIONS

Simplicity is always elegant if you are not sure how to go about decorating. The traditional white or pastel-colored table-cloths matching the bridesmaids' dresses may be just the touch needed. Remember that any shade of blue is attractive. Flowers may be added to the tables in low arrangements. (For more decorating ideas read the section entitled "Reception Flowers" in chapter 8.) Greenery or branches of flowering shrubbery may serve as a background for the receiving line. Festoons of twisted crepe-paper streamers and bells are still used, and can make the difference in a plain room for very little cost.

LIGHTING

Just as simple decorations can transform an otherwise plain room, lighting can also change the mood of a room significantly. Find out where the light switches are, and play with them ahead of time until you find the lighting to match the mood of your reception.

HOST AND HOSTESS

A host or hostess or a hospitality committee is an asset to have for the reception. Some churches have them oversee the whole wedding.

Before the ceremony, they should be there to meet the florist, the caterer, and the photographer, and to answer any questions these professionals may have.

After the recessional and before the guests are allowed to exit, the host may come to the front of the church to announce the procedure to follow. The guests will appreciate this direction. Otherwise, the host can make this announcement after everyone has arrived at the reception. The host and hostess will greet the guests at the door, and then direct

them to the receiving line and refreshment tables.

RECEPTION ASSISTANTS

Friends and relatives always feel honored to assist at the reception, even if it is a formal affair. Some of the duties they may be assigned are

- cutting the wedding cake (be sure they're experienced!)
- serving punch and coffee
- greeting guests and seeing that no one is left out
- attending the guest book

Send a note to these people about two weeks before the wedding to remind them of the date, time, and their particular responsibility. You may want to assign two or three different shifts of people.

Other assistance may be needed for:

- helping with decorations
- taking charge of the gifts
- passing our refreshments
- taking care of guests' coats
- cleaning up after the guests are served

MUSIC

Light music in the background will tend to make the wait in the lines more enjoyable. However, some rooms do not have very good acoustics, so it may just make the room noisier.

GUEST BOOK

Having a guest book to look through will help you remember the many friends and relatives who shared your special day.

If you are going to have it open at the ceremony, place it on a table near the entrance to the church and ask a friend to be the attendant. If you want to have it at the reception, you may ask the best man and maid of honor to be in charge of it. They can circulate among the guests gathering signatures.

Another alternative is to have the guest book at the end of the receiving line. However, you may miss some of the guests who attended the wedding only. If the tables are numbered, have the book located by the place where guests pick up their table cards.

GIFT TABLE

It is necessary to have a table set up to hold the gifts that are brought to the reception. It can be appropriately decorated with floor-length skirting or a white tablecloth.

PHOTOGRAPHER

If pictures are to be taken after the ceremony, the photographer should be given a limited amount of time to take pictures (twenty to thirty minutes should do). This way your guests will not be kept waiting too long.

THE RECEIVING LINE

The receiving line is optional, although most people still expect this tradition. Introductions of friends and relatives bring a natural warmth to the occasion. And the guests need to have an opportunity to express their congratulations and best wishes. It would be discourteous for guests not to make themselves known to the host and hostess.

For you, the receiving line is the ideal way to welcome each guest and express your joy at his or her presence. If the wedding is large, it may be the only time you will see each guest personally.

There are no longer any set rules as to who should stand in the receiving line. You may have the entire wedding party, or just the bride, groom, and both sets of parents. Traditionally, however, the receiving line is composed of the bride, groom, parents, and bridesmaids. If time is an element, a short line without the bridesmaids or with just the maid of honor and the best man is appropriate. This will free the rest to mingle with the guests.

Nowadays, with so many marriages breaking apart, we feel that the presence of both sets of parents in the receiving line is very significant. It is a sign of family unity, and of support for the newly married couple. We feel that this is especially appropriate in the context of a Christian wedding.

Usually your mother, as hostess of the reception, stands first. (This is true even with divorced parents.) It is her privilege to welcome each guest and introduce them to the groom's parents. If your mother doesn't know many of the guests, she may request someone to stand at her side to introduce each guest.

If your mother is deceased, your father stands at the beginning of the receiving line. He may ask a woman relative to stand with him, such as a grandmother, sister, or aunt.

The groom's parents stand next to your mother. It makes no difference who stands next to your mother—his father or his mother. But for appearance's sake, it is usually the groom's father.

If the groom's parents are divorced, only his mother stands in the receiving line, unless his father has not remarried, in which case the mother may consent to his standing in the receiving line also.

Your father is next, beside you, so he may introduce the guests to the new "Mr. and Mrs."

You should stand on the groom's right. Custom dictates that you should be greeted first, before the groom. If your groom is in the military, however, you should stand on his left and the receiving line should form in the opposite direction.

The maid of honor follows the groom. The bridesmaids line up after her, in the order of the wedding processional (see diagram). The ushers never stand in the receiving line, but may be close by.

There are several reasons for a father not to stand in the receiving line, one of which has already been mentioned—if the groom's father has divorced and remarried. Another exception would be if you and your groom are hosting the wedding, and you choose not to have the fathers stand in the receiving line. If this is the case, they may simply mingle with the guests.

The last reason why a father would not be present in the line is if the reception is

held in a home where space is limited. He may then choose to greet the guests at the door.

Another way to handle a space problem is to have the mother greet guests at the door, while you, your groom, and the maid of honor are in another corner, with the fathers nearby. Or, if you and your groom are hosting the wedding, the two of you may stand by the entrance.

Handicapped parents or ones in ill health may still take their rightful place in the line if they are seated comfortably.

A receiving line is unnecessary for a wedding with less than fifty guests. In this instance the couple may wander among the guests, greeting and chatting as they go.

Location of the Receiving Line
The location of the receiving line will depend on the size of the reception room. The line should be arranged so that there is space at both the beginning and at the end for the waiting guests. Chairs should be provided for the elderly, and punch provided. The best arrangement would be for the receiving line to be on one side in the middle of the room. However, it could be near the entrance, if the line does not have to go outside or up stairs. Regardless, try to hold the receiving line in the same room as the reception. Otherwise the guests might feel fragmented and anxious.

A receiving line in a garden is nice. But be sure to use insect repellant beforehand, as bees are attracted by bright colors and flowers.

When to Have the Receiving Line
It is more exciting if the receiving line can be held immediately after the wedding

RECEIVING LINE

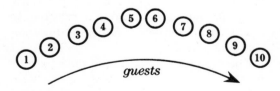

1. Bride's mother
2. Groom's father
3. Groom's mother
4. Father of bride
5. Bride
6. Groom
7. Maid of honor
8. Bridesmaid
9. Bridesmaid
10. Bridesmaid

while the spell of the ceremony is still upon everyone, than if it's formed at a reception that is held elsewhere.

If the wedding is attended by one hundred to one hundred fifty guests, the line can be formed in the narthex of the church. The guests may be greeted as they leave the sanctuary.

If you're having a church reception, it's best if you and your groom can slip away for a moment following the ceremony while the guests are directed to the reception room and offered punch and appetizers. After everyone is there, you and the groom may then appear to form the receiving line. In this way, no one will be held up on the steps or waiting in the sanctuary very long.

The cake may be served any time after you and the groom have cut it. It is not wise to detain the cutting of the cake, either, as some guests will have to leave. If the wedding has many guests, the receiving line may have to be interrupted. Otherwise, it can be done before the receiving line begins, with the best man or reception host making a few announcements at this time to explain the order of the reception.

In the case of a buffet meal, the cake is cut for dessert. If at all possible, try to be in the room before the food is served.

Photography is another factor in the timing of the receiving line. The proceedings will flow more smoothly if the majority of your pictures have been taken before the wedding. Otherwise, you might consider cutting the cake immediately after the ceremony, returning to the sanctuary for the photography session, and then forming the receiving line. However, you will always lose guests when you are away from the reception for any length of time.

An Unusual Receiving Line

If there is any awkward situation (such as divorced or handicapped parents) and you feel it best to avoid the usual receiving line, you may choose to do things somewhat differently.

After the recessional is complete, you and the groom may go back up the center aisle to serve as ushers. As the guests exit their pews, you may greet each person. This procedure keeps you and the groom in full view of the rest of the guests, and generally moves people out quickly.

SEATING ARRANGEMENTS

The Bridal Table

At a formal reception, the bridal table is usually a long table on one side of the reception room. It is skirted on the side facing the guests, and may be decorated with candles and flowers. Sometimes the bride's and bridesmaids' bouquets are placed on it for decoration. Place cards should indicate where each person is to sit.

You and your groom will sit in the center, facing the guests. You sit on the groom's right with the best man on your left. The maid of honor sits on the groom's left, and the ushers and bridesmaids are seated alternately on either side (see diagram). Any spouses may be included. As space is usually limited, however, spouses may be seated elsewhere.

At a small wedding, parents may also sit at the bride's table. Other family members and relatives may be seated nearby at a sit-down dinner.

It is not necessary to have a formal bride's table if you and your groom prefer to mingle with the guests. A table should

BRIDAL TABLE

PARENTS' TABLE

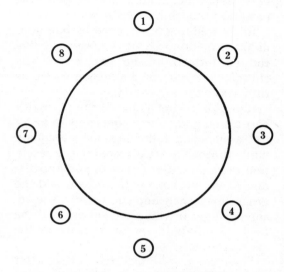

1. Bridesmaid
2. Groomsman
3. Bridesmaid
4. Best man
5. Bride
6. Groom
7. Maid of honor
8. Groomsman
9. Bridesmaid
10. Groomsman

still be reserved for you, however, so that the bridal party attendants may be seated if they wish.

The Parents' Table

This table may be set up even when there are no tables set up for the guests. At this table are seated both sets of parents, the grandparents, the minister and spouse, and any distinguished guests or close friends. Again place cards are important here.

There is a particular way the parents should be seated. The groom's mother sits on your father's right, and the groom's father sits on your mother's right. The minister would sit on your mother's left. The rest of the guests may be seated as desired (see diagram).

Note: Divorced parents would never be seated at the same table. They should be at separate tables with particular friends.

Bitterness and tension have no place at a wedding. The joy of celebration has often melted the hardest of hearts in seemingly unforgivable situations. Mothers and fathers overlook their grievances for a day and forgive what is in the past. Who knows—with God's help, it may be

1. Bride's father
2. Minister's wife
3. Friend or grandparent
4. Groom's father
5. Bride's mother
6. Minister
7. Friend or grandparent
8. Groom's mother

that healing will take place for a lifetime. Let's pray to that end.

The Guest Tables

At a formal reception, tables are numbered. The guests pick up numbered place cards as they enter. Otherwise, a waiter or friend could stand near the receiving line with a list, directing the guests to assigned tables.

If a buffet is served, the guests may be seated anywhere. In other situations, chairs may be set up in semicircles or against the walls.

The Cake Table

The person in charge of cutting the cake should be able to get to all sides of the cake. Therefore, it would be best to have the cake placed on a round table. A steady lazy-susan may also be used for easier handling.

In order to keep the cake table as neat as possible, two helpers are needed: one to hold the plates as the cake is cut, and the other to pick up the mess and take the dividers to the kitchen. This person should bring clean cloths out periodically for cleaning the knife.

The table should have a floor-length skirt. Additional decorations can be attached to the sides. The top should be kept free for setting out the plates of cake. A five-foot table will generally provide the needed space.

RECEPTION FLOOR PLAN AND TRAFFIC PATTERN

Now that you know the different tables and things that you'll need set up, a reception floor plan and traffic flow need to be determined.

In the space provided, sketch out the shape of your reception hall, indicating doorways, windows, electrical outlets, and other unalterable factors. Look through the sample buffet reception floor plans and traffic patterns included in this chapter to glean working ideas for your own plan. Perhaps you may even be able to use one of them without variation.

In your diagram, include tables for the bridal party, parents, guests, punch, food, and gifts. If tables are not being used for the guests, other seating arrangements will need to be made. Arrange the tables in an orderly fashion, allowing for an obvious traffic pattern. The traffic pattern should flow from the entrances to any lines (i.e., receiving, buffet) and then to available seating. Even if the best man or master of ceremonies is going to announce what the flow of traffic should be, it should not be so complicated that the guests cannot follow it with a minimum of instruction.

The placement of the receiving line and any musicians must also be considered.

BUFFET RECEPTION FLOOR PLANS

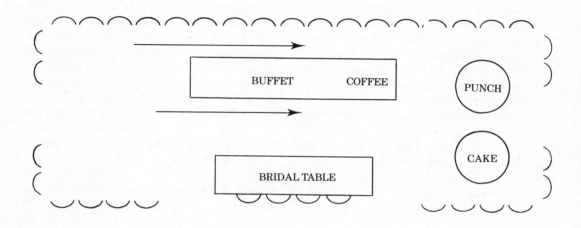

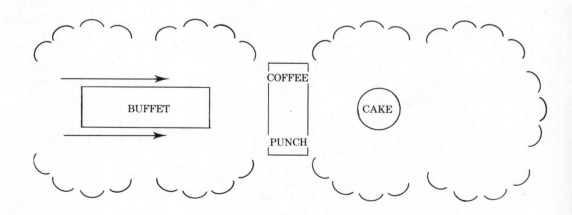

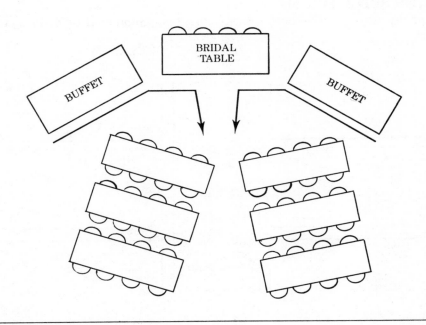

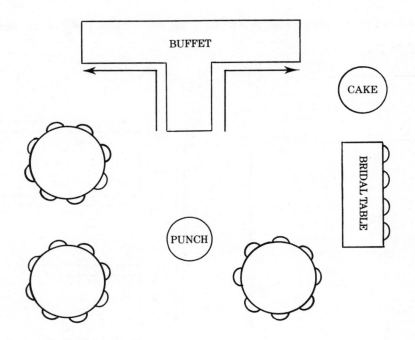

RECEPTION SETUP FOR 200

(Have same layout of food on both tables, using two-gallon chafing dishes, etc.)

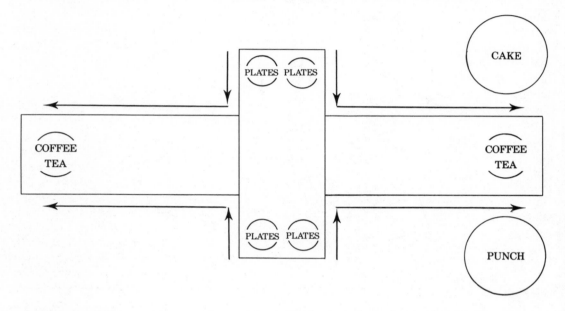

Alternative plan—Two tables end to end with plates in same position in center

RECEPTION TEA FOR 300

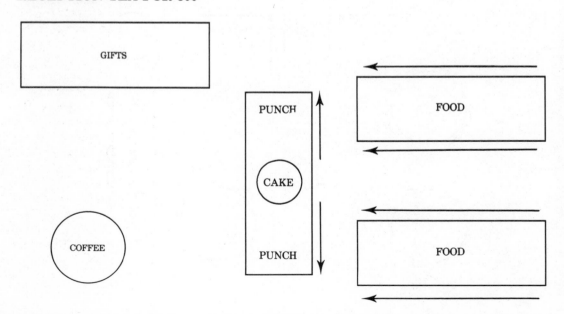

CUTTING THE CAKE

Use a sharp, thin knife. Insert the point straight down into the cake and then slice, pulling the knife toward you. Wipe off frosting with a warm, damp cloth.

Special instructions are needed for someone inexperienced in cutting a tiered cake, whether round or square. Begin by cutting the bottom layer around the edge of the layer above it. Then cut this portion of the first layer into wedges (or slices, if a square cake). When this is completed, cut the second layer around the edges of the third, and cut this into wedges. Continue in this fashion for each layer. Then return back to the bottom layer, slicing again along the new outer edge of the second layer. Remaining layers or the leftover cores of the larger round layers may be cut into wedges, diamonds, or slices, depending upon the size of the circle (see the diagrams below).

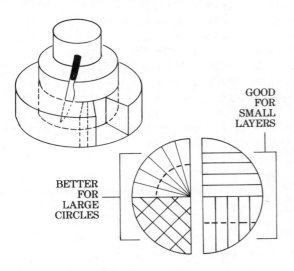

GOOD
FOR
SMALL
LAYERS

BETTER
FOR
LARGE
CIRCLES

Traditionally, the top layer is saved for the bride and groom's first anniversary. To save the cake top or any leftovers, place them in the freezer overnight (cover them if it's a frost-free freezer or else they'll dry out). The next day, remove the pieces, wrap them in plastic wrap, place in a box, and wrap the box. (An airtight container can be used instead of the box.)

THE CATERER

Professional catering is a hard job with much stress. Caterers often work twelve hours straight without a break to prepare for a meal. Forty to sixty hours are usually spent preparing food for two hundred guests. This hourly figure depends on the food served, the speed of the persons helping, and whether they know what they are doing or not. Caterers must pay their help well above minimum wage in order to get adequate help. But hiring a professional is worth it. A caterer's services usually include buying the food, cooking it, cleaning up, and providing the serving help that is needed. Most people are unaware of what they are paying for when the caterer gives them an estimate. They think it must be easy work for the caterer because he is experienced. However, it isn't, and a caterer often makes only a small profit.

Tell the caterer what you have budgeted to spend so he can work within that framework. He will need to know the style of your reception, the number of guests you expect, what facilities are available, and the preferred arrangement for serving and timing. Talk over the menu and let the caterer know if anyone is bringing anything special (such as breads, candies, canapés, smoked salmon, etc.). Find out if he will supply napkins and prepare the tables. (Paper plates and cups should not be used for a sit-down dinner.) Then he can give you a quote per person of what the meal will cost you.

Some caterers work out of their homes and call themselves "cooks." They do not charge as much for their services. You are fortunate if you know someone like this who can do your reception. Otherwise, choose someone who has a good reputation and is trusted by his clients. If you have hired a popular caterer, your guests will have all the more reason to look forward to the reception.

At least a week before the wedding, you will need to give the caterer a definite number of guests attending. Try not to have too many surprises for the caterer at the last minute. As has been said before, you can expect about two-thirds of the invited guests to attend. This will give you some guidelines as you plan with your caterer.

Some caterers and restaurants make it known that they intend to charge gratuities or tips *in addition* to their fees. Expect to tip the caterer 1 percent to 15 percent if he has offered special services, 15 percent to servers, including waitresses and waiters, and 15 percent to any driver, e.g., florist, limousine, etc.

SERVING

You and your groom should always be served first if there is waiter service. The attendants and parents would be next. If a buffet is being served, plates of food are brought to you, while everyone else serves themselves. Someone should be appointed to take care of people who may need special attention, such as elderly grandparents. They may need someone to arrange chairs for them and bring their food. The caterer should not be depended upon for this.

SPEECHES AND PROGRAMS

Usually some time during the reception the best man will gain everyone's attention. It may be in order to announce the arrival of the bridal party, or just to make necessary announcements and read messages of congratulations that arrived during the day. He could ask questions of the guests, such as, Who came the farthest? and Who is most recently engaged? Or he might give a speech of congratulations before you and the groom cut the cake.

If the best man is on the shy or quiet side, you may want to select someone else to serve as master of ceremonies, even though this is traditionally the best man's job. He should be able to make light, humorous comments while keeping the program moving.

A microphone could be set up so that family members could offer their wishes for happiness or, as the bride and groom, you may want to take this time to thank your parents and attendants. You may even have some guests present who would like to share gifts of music.

If a more extensive program is the custom, don't let it get out of hand with lengthy speeches from many people. Each speech should be limited to two minutes and should be prepared ahead of time. Even if you have planned the program to be short, it will go longer than you expect.

Slides of your childhoods can be interesting and fun. However, the presentation should be kept very short as some of the guests may not know you or the groom very well, and may become bored.

TOSSING THE BRIDE'S BOUQUET

Sometime before you leave the reception, the young unmarried women will gather around you to catch your bouquet. This tradition is followed to determine who will be the next to marry. Most likely you will have a special small bouquet to throw so that you can preserve the original one.

Turn your back to the women and toss the flowers up in the air, over your shoulder. Make sure the cameras are ready to catch a shot of the lucky girl grabbing the bouquet.

TOSSING THE GARTER

This oftentimes is not done at Christian weddings. This ancient tradition takes place after the tossing of the bouquet. Your groom removes the garter from your leg (you have it placed below your knee). The groom turns his back and throws it over his shoulder into the group of waiting bachelors. Whoever catches it is supposedly the next to wed.

A MOST UNUSUAL RECEPTION

One family served their guests an elegant wedding breakfast at ten-thirty in the morning. The menu consisted of:

EGG-CHEESE SOUFFLÉ CASSEROLE

POTATO SAUSAGE

FRUIT PLATE

FRUIT JELL-O MOLD

LIMPA (SWEDISH RYE BREAD)

BLUEBERRY MUFFINS

CARDAMOM COFFEE CAKE

COFFEE

After the breakfast, an explanation was given by the clergyman as to the plan and meaning of the wedding for the guests.

Then everyone went to the sanctuary for a worship service and wedding ceremony of great significance. Worship was emphasized through the union of Christ with the Christian home. After the noon wedding, the receiving line was held in the church parlor. Cake and punch were served at that time. The entire celebration was over by two-thirty in the afternoon.

The events of the day made the guests feel important and that their presence was highly desired. The parents placed their guests' comfort as the highest priority, and shared the best they had. They followed the principle of entertaining in the style that was the most enjoyable for their family and their friends. Love, affection, and selflessness were obvious on this day of days.

While somewhat less than traditional, this style of reception gave this particular family the balance they desired for the day. It fulfilled the purpose of the celebration and placed the reception in its proper perspective, with the wedding as the focal point.

Certainly this type of wedding reception would not be for everyone. Neither would a banana split reception or a soup and salad reception. However, consideration of the following principles, as well as a hard look at the budget, are of primary importance:

- the comfort of the guests
- the unselfish attitude of the bridal couple
- claiming the style that fits you
- the proper place of the reception in relationship to the Christian wedding
- a reasonable reception budget (see below)

RECEPTION COSTS

	ESTIMATED	ACTUAL
Cost of room rental	$ _____	$ _____
Caterer	_____	_____
Food	_____	_____
Beverage	_____	_____
Cake	_____	_____
Decorations	_____	_____
Flowers	_____	_____
Assistants	_____	_____
Gratuities	_____	_____
Total	$ _____	$ _____

WEDDING DAY RECEPTION AGENDA

Include such things as prepare the food, cook, serve, receiving line, cut and serve the cake, throw bouquet, throw garter, etc.

TIME	ACTIVITY
_____	_____
_____	_____
_____	_____
_____	_____
_____	_____
_____	_____
_____	_____
_____	_____
_____	_____
_____	_____
_____	_____

CHURCH WEDDING RECEPTION WORKSHEET

Date _____ Time _____ to _____

Estimated number of guests _____

Caterer _____ Phone _____

Host and hostess _____ Phone _____

ASSIGNMENTS:

Shop

_____

_____

Prepare food

_____

_____

Cook

_____

Prepare, replenish, and clean up punch

_____

Prepare, replenish, and clean up coffee, tea

_____

_____

Replenish buffet

_____

_____

Serve full meal

_____

_____

_____

Cut and serve cake

_____

_____

_____

Decorate

_____

_____

_____

Set up and take down tables and chairs

_____

_____

Clean up

_____

_____

_____

_____

Servers: Attendants:

punch _____   greeters _____
                          guest book
_____
                          _____
_____
coffee, tea   gift table

_____   coats _____
                          other _____
_____

_____   _____

_____   _____

_____   _____

MASTER RECEPTION ASSISTANTS' LIST						
ASSISTANTS	PHONE	ASSIGNMENT	TIME TO ARRIVE	REMINDER SENT OR PHONED	THANK-YOU NOTE SENT	GIFT, DONATION, TIP

Homemade Reception Plans

You may be the type who derives great satisfaction from making everything for the reception yourself. Or, you may be forced to do this to cut down on expenses. Whatever the case, it *can* be done. The secret is to be well organized and have plenty of help. The forms and worksheets in the preceding chapter will be invaluable.

It is important for you to read entirely through the preceding chapter to get a clear idea of what is involved with a reception. For instance, the previous section on "Reception Assistants" will give you a list of the duties that can be delegated to friends and relatives. "The Caterer" section gives a glimpse of the duties a professional caterer can be counted on to carry out. If you are planning to do your reception without the help of professionals, *you* will become the caterer.

Extra help is imperative at any party, and a wedding reception is no exception. If you have a particular married couple you are close to, you may ask them to serve as the head supervisors. On the day of the wedding, you may then confidently leave all the details to them.

Some of your other friends may be willing to assist also. Write them a personal note or phone them, asking them to assist you with a particular duty. Also specify the dates and times they would be needed. But hire someone to do the dishes, if possible, since this is not an honorable task!

Keep the Master Reception Assistants' List (chapter 21) by the phone so that you will have easy access to this list if any changes need to be made. Give a duplicate copy of the list to your supervising couple.

Arrange for a "rehearsal" of the reception a few days before the wedding. This will give everyone an opportunity to ask questions, run through the details, and check supplies.

The following sections will take a closer look at the details you will need to arrange for.

FOOD GUIDELINES

Quantities

For a wedding reception tea, allow four to six small sandwiches and two cookies per person. For light refreshments, you will probably need 300 to 500 pieces of food for fifty guests. This would involve small sandwiches, a relish tray, and fruit plate.

The amount of beverage you will need depends on the time of year and the time of day your wedding is held. Here are some figures to keep in mind as you plan: Average about two 4-ounce cups of punch per hour per person; two pounds of coffee per 100 guests; one pint of cream; and a half pound of sugar. For punch, consider using fruit juice concentrate and carbonated beverage in an economical fifty-fifty proportion.

Go to the library and find a cookbook for large groups. Recipes for eight or ten do not always multiply well.

The amount of a stew-type dish (such as Chicken a la King) for a 100-guest buffet supper would be five to six gallons. The same would be true for fruit salad. You can also calculate this at one gallon per 20 guests, or one cup per person. Four pounds each of nuts and mints for 100 guests should be enough. It's always better to have more than is needed.

Shopping

The most important thing to remember is to allow yourself plenty of time when shopping for the food items. Look for bargains if your budget is limited. Be flexible, because exactly what you have planned may not be available. But something else will do just as well. Have a place to store all of the items that you have purchased.

For fresh food, watch for sales on the weekend of the wedding. The discount markets do not necessarily have better prices.

If you are going to serve chicken, consider buying whole chickens for the breast and thigh meat; it is less expensive than buying the separate pieces. Freeze the wings and backs for another time.

The deli in many stores will make almost anything you want, from a hot ham to a roast turkey. They also have party finger sandwiches with assorted fillings and cold buffet platters with meat and cheeses. Remember the bakery outlets for reasonable dinner rolls.

Keep accurate record of your needs with the Reception Shopping List.

EQUIPMENT

Once the menu has been decided on you can determine the presently available equipment you will be using. List the items *you* will need to supply on the Reception Shopping List. Also look into the matter of chairs and tables. Will you need to find more of each?

One way to keep yourself organized is to have several charts pinned to the wall in the kitchen. Use the Wedding Day Reception Agenda for the timing (preparing, cooking, serving, cutting the cake, cleaning up, etc.), another chart for seating arrangements, and another one showing special table arrangements. It will be best to have a diagram of the lighting and electrical outlets also.

RECEPTION SHOPPING LIST

Date _____ Time _____

Menu

MENU INGREDIENTS	QUANTITY NEEDED	COST	EQUIPMENT FOR PREPARATION	BUY	BORROW OR RENT	COST
		$				$
Beverage						
Miscellaneous						
	Total	$ ═══			Total	$ ═══

EQUIPMENT CHECKLIST

After you have completed this checklist, transfer the items you will need to the Reception Shopping List.

Date _____ Time _____ Rental Fee _____

EQUIPMENT:	HAVE	NEED
Punch bowls		
Cups		
Ladle		
Cake knife		
Coffee service		
Tea		
Coffee		
Creamer		
Sugar		
Silverware		
Platters, trays		
Serving utensils		
Dinnerware		
China		
Glass		
Disposable		
Glassware		
Disposable		
Tablecloths		
Candelabra, vases		
Tables for:		
Bridal party		
Parents		
Guests		
Cake		
Punch		
Gifts		
Guest book		
Skirts, pins, ribbons		
Coat rack		
Microphone		
Tent		
Paper goods, napkins		
Towels, detergent		
Other:		

FOOD PREPARATION

Sandwiches should always be made on the morning of the wedding. In some areas, all the relatives gather at the church to make the sandwiches together. They make quite a party of it. The ingredients will have been previously purchased by the bride or her parents.

Fruit breads can be made weeks ahead and frozen. Package mixes are a great help in terms of time, measuring, and shopping. Meatballs and chicken for salad can easily be prepared ahead of time and frozen. The meatballs may then be heated in a roaster with or without a barbeque or sweet and sour sauce. Adding pineapple and sunflower seeds to chicken salad makes it interesting.

SERVING

The serving logistics for a wedding reception with light refreshments for 100 guests would necessarily involve one or two people in the kitchen, one or two to serve the beverage, and four to serve the cake and other refreshments. For a seated meal for the same number of guests, it would be helpful to have twelve to serve and three in the kitchen. For a buffet, you would need eight persons to supply the buffet and two in the kitchen. More help would be needed for a larger number of guests.

Try to have a separate staff for the punch and coffee table: one person to make, replenish, and clean up the punch; and one person to do the same for the coffee. Others would do the serving.

If a buffet is served, foods should be placed from right to left in the order of a regular menu (i.e., appetizers, entrees, vegetables, salads, and sweets). When it is possible, place the main dishes on a higher level for easier accessibility. This looks nicer, also. If guests are not to be seated at tables, serve food that does not have to be cut.

Paper plates are never as nice as glass or china, but if you have to borrow or rent in order to have glass or china, consider the time involved in picking up, unpacking, washing, packing, and returning the dishes. If you do decide to go with paper products and are having a buffet for 100 guests, buy 200 paper plates and napkins, 150 knives, forks, and spoons, with extras for dessert.

If the food is disappearing rapidly, the eating time can be shortened by starting any planned programs or by cutting the cake. This need often arises when the pictures are taken after the ceremony or when the receiving line is very long.

CAKE

Start making the decorations for your wedding cake a week ahead of time. Bake the cake in advance and freeze it. Assembling it should not take place any earlier than twenty-four hours before the reception. You will need a steady board to build it on.

When you figure the cost of the ingredients, you may find you are not saving as much as you had hoped. It may be easier to hire a baker for this job.

THE BANANA SPLIT RECEPTION

If you want to do something really different, try a reception like this: banana splits for 300 guests!

Make ice cream balls ahead of time and freeze.

Decorate seven round tables with skirts to the floor. For each table fill a punch bowl with ice cream balls and place in the center. Place bowls of bananas and toppings (strawberry, butterscotch, etc.) around the punch bowl. Also have nuts, marshmallows, cherries, etc., available.

Decorate whipped cream cans with fabric or paper to match your color scheme.

Purchase or rent banana split dishes.

You may still have a wedding cake (preferably carrot cake) and fruit punch.

DECORATIONS

Instead of buying tablecloths for the cake and punch tables, you may choose to make them yourself. Here are three different ideas for skirting the tables.

Make the skirt out of satin or other material. Measure the length from the table top to the floor to make sure your material is wide enough. The skirt should be double the circumference of the table. Make a three-inch hem at the bottom and a one-inch casing at the top. Then insert a drawstring through the casing. Place the skirt around the table and pull the drawstring. Straight pins can be used to hold the gathers in place. Next, pin the end of a strand of one-inch wide ribbon over the casing. Run it along about four inches, pin it, fold it back against the ribbon, and pin again through both ribbons at about one inch. Go forward again about four inches, pin, turn back against ribbon, pin at one inch, and go forward. (Pins should go up and down.) Repeat this all the way around the table. This will put a nice finishing touch to the top edge.

Or, use colored sheets as floor-length tablecloths and then drape lace fabric in swags around the sides. Accented with ribbons or little flowers where the swags are tacked up, this can make a beautiful table!

Another idea for table skirtings would be to purchase lengths of florist paper. This is the decorative paper used to wrap plants. It comes in many colors and shades. It is usually the same width as the length from table top to floor. An edging of ribbon or lace ruffling can finish it off.

RICE BAGS

To make little rice bags, cut a five-inch square of netting and a seven-inch length of ribbon for each bag. Fill each square with a tablespoon of rice or birdseed, and tie securely with the ribbon.

Or, for a more elegant touch, make satin flowers in which to place birdseed or rice. Pink the edges of 4½-by-3-inch pieces of satin. Sew the short sides together and attach one end with floral tape to a six-inch piece of floral wire. (An artificial green leaf can be taped on to each stem for a natural look.) Place birdseed or rice in the tops of the "flowers" and then fold down the open ends about one inch into the center.

The rice bags or flowers can be passed out to the guests either before the bride and groom leave the church (on their way to the reception) or just before the couple leaves the reception.

Intimacy & the Honeymoon

PREPARING FOR THE HONEYMOON

Many couples have found this triangle diagram helpful in viewing their spiritual relationships.

The diagrams below clearly depict how their individual spiritual relationships with God affect their relationship with each other. If you and your groom both grow close to God, you will also draw close to one another.

If you fall away, you likewise move away from each other. If one draws close to God and the other does not, the distance remains.

So it is of the greatest importance that you and your groom learn to maintain an authentic closeness to God. There is nothing more important in Christian marriage than this.

However, you should be careful to avoid the very human tendency to pretend spirituality in the hope that God will bless your marriage. It is quite common for a bride or groom to become very spiritual as the wedding approaches—and then after the wedding, fall back to his or her original state of disinterest. Guard your hearts; be honest with God and each other. Never hesitate to contact your pastor or a mature Christian friend about your spiritual life.

During the engagement period many couples begin the practice of having their devotions together. This is commendable as long as these devotional times do not replace individual Bible reading and prayer.

Some couples purchase and read copies of the same books. Some couples pray for similar items on their prayer lists. Others read the same Scripture passages daily. One way to "count down" the days to the wedding is to read the Psalms in descending order. For instance, if there are sixty days until the wedding, read Psalm 60, the next day, Psalm 59, continuing down to Psalm 1 for the wedding day.

PRACTICAL ARRANGEMENTS

It is very important that you and the groom avoid being worn out as your wedding day approaches. If you are exhausted, you both may not get off to the best start on your wedding night. Plan to have all the wedding preparations taken care of at least two weeks before the wedding, and don't stay up too late the night before the wedding. It is wise to schedule an early wedding rehearsal and dinner.

Some precautions are in order for choosing a place to spend the first night. Do not arrange for a hotel that is far away, because this will require long traveling. And, if at all possible, arrange to see the room you are going to rent. Remember that privacy is of the utmost importance.

Be careful not to plan too many events for your honeymoon. This time should be spent getting to know each other. This will not happen if you pass from one tour to another.

PREPARING FOR SEXUAL INTIMACY

The act of intercourse is a uniting of two people in a form of communication that is absolutely unique. The nature of this form of communication leaves one extremely vulnerable; you have to leave yourself open in order to communicate in a sexual relationship. And a sexual relationship with this degree of openness does not come simply with a ring or the first intercourse. It takes time for it to grow. It should be better after five years, after twenty years, even after forty years. There is no such thing as a stagnant human relationship. You are either increasing or decreasing in a relationship, and the sexual part of marriage goes along with the other aspects; it has to develop.

Sexual intercourse is an important part of a male-female marriage relationship. It is ordained by God. It is considered ac-

ceptable behavior by God. This relationship does not occur in a satisfactory form just because one is male and one is female. The sexual relationship, to a certain extent, involves one's whole life. One *cannot* put sex in a corner, pull it out for an hour or so, and yet never respond emotionally with the spouse the rest of the day or week. A successful sexual relationship is the culmination of work, time, words said, and hours of learning about each other.

Dr. Stewart Odell, an obstetrician and gynecologist for over twenty years, offers some straightforward advice to couples about preparation for sexual intimacy.

Dr. Odell believes the engaged couple should have physical examinations before the wedding to insure that their physical characteristics are normal. For the male, the exam should include a serology (a form of blood test), a complete physical with particular attention to the genital area (penis and testes), and general counsel. For the female, the exam should include a serology and a general physical examination with special attention to the breast and pelvic areas, including the hymen (a membrane going partly across the opening of the vagina). If the hymen is excessively tight, it can be dilated or surgically cut to enlarge it before intercourse is attempted. This exam also gives the gynecologist a chance to give some basic counsel; to talk about the first sexual intercourse, contraception, and reasonable expectations within the marriage relationship, including physical, emotional, and psychological intimacy.

The premarital exam should also include a frank discussion of your first intercourse. There are many books on the market dealing with initial intercourse. Perhaps your pastor could recommend one to you. The initial act must be done gently, with concern for the other partner. Plenty of lubrication, such as KY jelly or Vaseline, should be used. Lay aside any preconceived ideas about how it will or should be. This individual act between two people is unique, and should be a learning experience for the life of the marriage. To learn the sexual act takes time. Each person has unique physical capacities, and in time, will learn to make the sexual act more enjoyable for his or her partner.

Sexually, the normal male response is much quicker than the female's. This is universal. But generally after you are married for a period of time this "gap" is narrowed (although not necessarily eliminated).

CONTRACEPTION

Some people have a hard time determining whether or not contraception is acceptable from a biblical perspective. Dr. Odell believes contraception *is* acceptable within the framework of God's will. God gave us an intellectual mind by which to make choices, and we are responsible for using it correctly. We are to use our mind and our choices to glorify Him.

If contraception is a possibility for you, you should be aware of the several forms available before choosing one.

Forms of Contraception

The *oral* contraceptive, "the pill," is 99.9 percent effective. The pill prevents ovulation; therefore, conception cannot occur. Certain possible side-effects are nausea, vomiting, headaches, emotional irritability, and increased chances of blood clots in the legs and lungs. You should *not* take the pill if you have had hepatitis within

[handwritten: more like 98%]

[handwritten: false!]

the last three years, you have a history of breast cancer, or you have a history of blood clots in the legs or lungs.

The *intrauterine* contraceptive device (IUD) is 98 to 99 percent effective. The IUD prevents the fertilized egg from implanting in the lining of the uterus. Side-effects could include breakthrough bleeding, and a greater chance of tubal pregnancy and/or infections in the fallopian tubes which could result in sterility. The IUD should *not* be used in women who have not had a previous pregnancy, in an abnormal uterus, or in the presence of infection in the uterus or fallopian tubes. The use of an IUD is *not recommended* because it is an abortive device which performs a *de facto* destruction of the united sperm and ovum.

The *diaphragm* is 95 to 96 percent effective. The diaphragm with a spermicidal jelly or cream on it works by destroying the sperm so that fertilization cannot take place. The possible side-effects are vaginal infections and allergic reactions. It should *not* be used if you have an unusual sized or shaped vagina.

Prophylactics or condoms are also 95 to 96 percent effective. There are no side-effects with this method. Everything relies on the male using it faithfully.

Contraceptive *gels, foams, sponges,* and *suppositories* are 94 to 95 percent effective. These contraceptives are made of chemicals which destroy the sperm in the vagina. The side-effects may be vaginal infections, vaginitis, and local allergic reactions.

The *rhythm* and/or *thermal* methods are 85 to 95 percent effective. They do not work well after delivery or if your menstrual periods are irregular. They have no side-effects, however, other than the comparative lack of effectiveness.

[handwritten bottom: The "pill" works via 3 mechanisms: prevention of ovulation, thickening of cervical mucous to impede sperm, and altering the uterine lining so that implantation of an ovulated and fertilized egg is not likely. This last mode of operation is clearly abortive and occurs from 2-50% of the time. It is a combination of these 3 mechanisms which accounts for the pill's effectiveness.]

Your physician can give you an explanation of these methods.

Coitus interruptus or withdrawal is 80 to 90 percent effective. While there are no side-effects, there can be a lack of sexual fulfillment.

If a couple does not use any form of contraception, there is an 85 to 90 percent chance that the female will be pregnant within twelve months. In other words, not using any contraceptive is 10 to 15 percent effective. You can see how your fertility rate is decreased dramatically with any of the above means.

ASSOCIATED MEDICAL PROBLEMS

There are several medical problems that might occur with a sexual relationship. You may get cystitis, a bladder infection which occurs because of the frequency of intercourse. Cystitis is characterized by frequent urination accompanied by pain or possibly even the presence of blood. It occurs because the bladder lining is not accustomed to intercourse. After a period of time the cystitis will not occur because the tissue becomes tougher and does not become inflamed. Cystitis needs to be treated with an antibiotic.

Vaginitis may also occur. This needs to be treated with a vaginal cream. The use of lubrication before intercourse will decrease this irritation.

There also may be some bleeding with the first intercourse because of the tearing of the hymenal area. This is usually self-limited and does not cause any real problem.

THE FIRST YEAR

Deuteronomy 24:5 suggests a principle that newlyweds should take to heart. It reads, "When a man takes a new wife, he shall not go out with the army, nor be charged with any duty; he shall be free at home one year and shall give happiness to his wife whom he has taken" (NASB). Evidently in the Hebrew economy great care was taken to allow a young couple time to get to know each other in their first year of marriage. If at all possible, it will be wise for you to do the same. The main reason is that during the first year patterns are set which will affect the months and years to come.

It is important, therefore, that you plan for times to get away. Some couples have sadly discovered when looking back over the first year that there were few dinners out and no nights away. We recommend that couples schedule overnight trips at least every five weeks during the first year of marriage. A night camping at a borrowed cabin, or a night at a hotel will allow for mental relaxation, rest, and time to understand your intimate life. You will probably not have a lot of money to spend on such times, so be creative. The less expensive times will be just as enjoyable as those high-priced outings.

Again, do not fall into the trap of expecting perfection in your sexual relationship in the first few years. By expecting too much, a perfectionistic husband or wife can sabotage what would otherwise have been a most satisfactory sexual relationship.

CHAPTER TWENTY FOUR

Your New Name

To the vast majority of people, "Mrs. John Smith" means you are married to a particular man. It may take a year or so before your old friends are used to referring to you by this new name. Eventually, though, this name will become a part of you. It is a symbol of you and your new husband joining as one. It is a cultural tradition, although not a law.

Some women today decide not to change their last names. They either have professional reasons or they may want to preserve their given identity. If you take this path, it is important to notify your friends of this decision. (You should expect some disagreement on this, also.)

Some women choose to use a dual identification, such as using one name on the occupational scene and one on the home front, or, a hyphenated husband/wife name. Be consistent with whatever name you choose for all legal work or financial dealings.

If you change your name, your signature should read: first name, maiden or middle name initial, and married last name. When signing friendly letters, use your first name only, or first name and married last name. Never sign "Mrs. John Smith." Instead, sign "Jane Smith" and then underneath you may put "(Mrs. John)."

If you have your own income you may wish to establish your own credit. Maintain your own bank account and have credit cards issued in your name rather than being designated as an "authorized user." This way if you ever need money (to start a business, etc.), you will have earned your own credit rating.

If you go out of the country for your honeymoon, bring along your marriage license and identification cards (such as driver's license, voter's registration, etc.) to avoid any problems with your passport.

The Illinois Bar Association puts out an excellent pamphlet containing various legal information. It is called "Advice to Newly Marrieds." You may obtain a copy by writing the Illinois Bar Association, Bar Center, Springfield, IL 62701. Other states' bar associations may also have a similar pamphlet.

WHEN CHANGING YOUR NAME, CHANGE YOUR . . .

WHAT	WHERE	WHAT YOU NEED TO DO
Bank accounts checking account savings account safe deposit box loans	Banks	Make out new signature cards.
Car registration	Sec'y of State Title Division	Bring in the title, registration, and marriage certificate or give information on preprinted form for license.
Driver's license	Sec'y of State	Write for form or go to nearby office with a certified copy of marriage certificate, your driver's license, and another identification.
Credit cards	Main office of store or company	Write a letter of request with your signature.
Insurance	Your agent	Make necessary changes on car, health, and life insurance. Change beneficiaries, effective the day after the wedding.
Taxes	On next return	Use new name and same social security number.
Legal papers leases pensions disability papers property titles	Your lawyer	
Magazines	Publishers	Advise of change six to eight weeks before wedding or make change at expiration date.
Mail delivery	Post office	Write a note to the postmaster.
Passport	Post office	Bring in passport and marriage certificate and they will send them with an amendment form to the passport office, which will send the changed passport and marriage license back to you.
Social Security card	U.S. Social Security Office	Send certified copy of your marriage certificate.
Stocks and bonds	Transfer agent	Execute a power of attorney.
School and employee records	Personnel, registrar, and alumni office	Notify of change of name to update records and mailings.
Voter's registration	City Hall Library Board of Elections	Reregister—also reregister if you move to another area.

Some other helpful suggestions for financial planning:
_____ Explore possible insurance options and change names, addresses, and beneficiaries, if agreeable.
_____ Making a will is a very sound and wise move before the wedding.
_____ See a tax consultant and look into your new tax status.

That special day that was uniquely planned just for the two of you is now past. As you begin a lifetime of making memories together, remember the vows you made in the presence of God and your friends and relatives.

Draw close to Christ, and as you genuinely do so, you will find that your sense of oneness will deepen. As you learn to share your inner thoughts with one another, consciously attempt to make deep, honest communication a pattern for your lives.

In your marriage, may you both strive to be more like Christ. Try to understand as though you were the other. Give up your own desires in the interest of the other. Live each for the other. Covenant, by God's grace, to make your deep love like Christ's—a shoreless, bottomless sea, which naturally flows to family, friends, and neighbors. And, again following the example of our Lord Jesus, continually lift up the other in prayer.

You and your beloved are now in the great springtime of your lives. Right now life for you involves many exciting, new beginnings. Use this excitement, along with the anticipation of what is to come, to get the most out of your marriage.

Ruth Muzzy
R. Kent Hughes

◆ N O T E S ◆

DATE DUE

NOV 1 9 1991	FEB 1 6 2004	
DEC 0 2 1991		
DEC 1 0 1991		
3 1991		
DEC 1 3 1991		
FEB 1 0 1992		
FEB 2 4 1992		
APR 27 1992		
AUG 2 1 1992		
OCT 1 9 1992		
NOV 0 2 1992		
FEB 1 9 1993		
MAR 1 6 1994		
NOV 2 5 1997		
JUN 2 5 1998		
APR 0 1 1999		
MAR 1 5 2002		